HOUSING ISSUES, LAWS AND PROGRAMS

MULTIFAMILY HOUSING

ACTIVITIES OF FANNIE MAE AND FREDDIE MAC

HOUSING ISSUES, LAWS AND PROGRAMS

Additional books in this series can be found on Nova's website under the Series tab.

Additional E-books in this series can be found on Nova's website under the E-book tab.

HOUSING ISSUES, LAWS AND PROGRAMS

MULTIFAMILY HOUSING

ACTIVITIES OF FANNIE MAE AND FREDDIE MAC

JACOB A. PEZZO
EDITOR

nova publishers
New York

For permission to use material from this book please contact us:
Telephone 631-231-7269; Fax 631-231-8175
Web Site: http://www.novapublishers.com

Library of Congress Cataloging-in-Publication Data

ISBN: 978-1-62417-654-8

Published by Nova Science Publishers, Inc. † New York

CONTENTS

PREFACE

Fannie Mae and Freddie Mac are charted by Congress as government-sponsored enterprises (GSEs) to provide liquidity in the mortgage market and promote homeownership for underserved groups and locations. They purchase mortgages, guarantee them, and package them in mortgage-backed securities (MBSs), which they either keep as investments or sell to institutional investors. This book examines Congressional interest in Fannie Mae and Freddie Mac which has increased in recent years, primarily because the federal government's continuing conservatorship of these GSEs, at a time of uncertainty in the housing, mortgage, and financial markets, has raised doubts about the future of the enterprises and the potential cost to the Treasury of guaranteeing the enterprises' debt. Since more than 60% of households are homeowners, a large number of citizens could be affected by the future of GSEs.

Chapter 1 - Congress established the enterprises to provide stability in the secondary market for residential mortgages and serve the mortgage credit needs of targeted groups. But in September 2008, FHFA placed the enterprises in conservatorship out of concern that their deteriorating financial condition would destabilize the financial system. As Congress and the Executive Branch have explored options for restructuring the enterprises, most of the discussion has focused on the single-family market. But the enterprises also play a large role in providing financing for multifamily properties (those with five or more units). GAO was asked to describe (1) how the enterprises' multifamily loan activities have changed, (2) the enterprises' role in the multifamily financing marketplace and how they met affordable housing goals, and (3) how the enterprises' multifamily delinquency rates compare with those of other mortgage capital sources and how they have managed their credit risk.

To address these objectives, GAO analyzed (1) loan-level data from 1994 (the earliest period for which loan-level data were available) through 2011 from the enterprises and (2) data from the Mortgage Bankers Association; interviewed key multifamily housing stakeholders; and reviewed FHFA examination reports. FHFA, Fannie Mae, and Freddie Mac provided technical comments, which GAO incorporated where appropriate.

Chapter 2 - Fannie Mae and Freddie Mac are charted by Congress as government-sponsored enterprises (GSEs) to provide liquidity in the mortgage market and promote homeownership for underserved groups and locations. They purchase mortgages, guarantee them, and package them in mortgage-backed securities (MBSs), which they either keep as investments or sell to institutional investors. In addition to the GSEs' guarantees, investors widely believe that MBSs are implicitly guaranteed by the federal government. In 2008, the GSEs financial condition had weakened and there were concerns over their ability to meet their obligations on $1.2 trillion in bonds and $3.7 trillion in MBSs that they had guaranteed. In response to the financial risks, the federal government took control of these GSEs in a process known as conservatorship as a means to stabilize the mortgage credit market.

Congressional interest in Fannie Mae and Freddie Mac has increased in recent years, primarily because the federal government's continuing conservatorship of these GSEs, at a time of uncertainty in the housing, mortgage, and financial markets, has raised doubts about the future of the enterprises and the potential cost to the Treasury of guaranteeing the enterprises' debt. Since more than 60% of households are homeowners, a large number of citizens could be affected by the future of the GSEs. Congress exercises oversight over the Federal Housing Finance Agency (FHFA), which is both regulator and conservator of the GSEs, and is considering legislation to shape the future of the GSEs.

Estimates of the eventual total cost to the federal government of supporting the GSEs use different baselines and vary widely. FHFA estimates that Treasury is likely to purchase $220 billion-$311 billion of senior preferred stock by the end of 2014. The Congressional Budget Office estimates the budget cost to be more than $300 billion. Standard & Poor's has estimated the cost at $280 billion plus $405 billion to create a replacement system.

Under terms of the federal government's support agreement as amended and effective on August 17, 2012, the enterprises will pay the Treasury all of their quarterly profits (if any). Under the previous agreements, the enterprises paid Treasury dividends of nearly $20 billion annually (10% of the support). Paying the federal government all profits earned in a quarter could prevent the

GSEs from accumulating funds to redeem the senior preferred stock. However, it would appear that the GSEs could make quarterly redemptions.

The financial condition of the GSEs appears to be improving. In the first and second quarters of 2012, both Fannie Mae and Freddie Mac reported profits for the first time since the fourth quarter of 2006. Also, the second quarter of 2012 was first time that neither GSE had to request financial support from the Treasury.

In: Multifamily Housing
Editor: Jacob A. Pezzo

ISBN: 978-1-62417-654-8

Chapter 1

MORTGAGE FINANCING: FANNIE MAE ANDFREDDIE MAC'S MULTIFAMILY HOUSING ACTIVITIES HAVE INCREASED*

United States Government Accountability Office

ABBREVIATIONS

ACLI	American Council of Life Insurers
activity report	Annual Housing Activity Report
AMI	area median income
ARM	adjustable-rate mortgage
CMBS	commercial mortgage-backed security
CREFC	Commercial Real Estate Finance Council
DUS®	Delegated Underwriting and Servicing
enterprise	government-sponsored enterprise
Federal Reserve System	Board of Governors of the Federal Reserve
FDIC	Federal Deposit Insurance Corporation
FHA	Federal Housing Administration

* This is an edited, reformatted and augmented version of The United States Government Accountability Office publication, Report to the Chairman, Committee on Financial Services, House of Representatives, GAO-12-849, dated September 2012.

FHFA	Federal Housing Finance Agency
HERA	Housing and Economic Recovery Act of 2008
HFA	housing finance agency
HUD	Department of Housing and Urban Development
LIHTC	low-income housing tax credit
LTV	loan-to-value
MBA	Mortgage Bankers Association
MBS	mortgage-backed security
MSA	metropolitan statistical area
NAAHL	National Association of Affordable Housing Lenders
NCSHA	National Council of State Housing Agencies
NIBP	New Issue Bond Program
OFHEO	Office of Federal Housing Enterprise Oversight
REO	real estate-owned
RHS	Rural Housing Service
Safety and Soundness Act	Federal Housing Enterprises Financial Safety and Soundness Act of 1992
TCLF	Temporary Credit and Liquidity Facilities
Treasury	Department of the Treasury

WHY GAO DID THIS STUDY

Congress established the enterprises to provide stability in the secondary market for residential mortgages and serve the mortgage credit needs of targeted groups. But in September 2008, FHFA placed the enterprises in conservatorship out of concern that their deteriorating financial condition would destabilize the financial system. As Congress and the Executive Branch have explored options for restructuring the enterprises, most of the discussion has focused on the single-family market. But the enterprises also play a large role in providing financing for multifamily properties (those with five or more units).

GAO was asked to describe (1) how the enterprises' multifamily loan activities have changed, (2) the enterprises' role in the multifamily financing marketplace and how they met affordable housing goals, and (3) how the enterprises' multifamily delinquency rates compare with those of other mortgage capital sources and how they have managed their credit risk.

To address these objectives, GAO analyzed (1) loan-level data from 1994 (the earliest period for which loan-level data were available) through 2011 from the enterprises and (2) data from the Mortgage Bankers Association; interviewed key multifamily housing stakeholders; and reviewed FHFA examination reports.

FHFA, Fannie Mae, and Freddie Mac provided technical comments, which GAO incorporated where appropriate.

WHAT GAO FOUND

From 1994 through 2011, the multifamily loan activities of Fannie Mae and Freddie Mac (the enterprises) generally increased. In this period, Fannie Mae held a lower percentage of multifamily loans in its portfolio than Freddie Mac. While the enterprises' multifamily business operations generally were profitable, both enterprises reported losses in 2008 and 2009.

In recent years, Fannie Mae and Freddie Mac played a larger role in the multifamily marketplace, and their multifamily activities contributed considerably to meeting their affordable housing goals (set by their regulator for the purchase of mortgages that serve targeted groups or areas). Before 2008, the enterprises financed about 30 percent of multifamily loans (see figure).

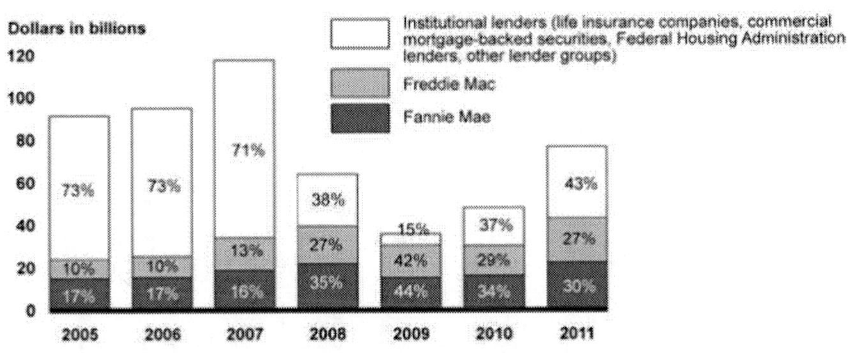

Source: GAO analysis of Mortgage Bankers Assosiation data.
Note: Percentages may not add to 100 because of rounding.

Financing of Multifamily Loans Originated, 2005-2011.

Their share increased to 86 percent in 2009, but decreased to 57 percent in 2011 as other participants reentered the market. GAO's analysis showed that multifamily activities greatly contributed to the enterprises' ability to meet affordable housing goals. For example, the enterprises' multifamily activities constituted 4.5 percent of their total business in 2008, but about a third of the units used to meet the goal of serving low- and moderate-income persons were multifamily units.

The enterprises have purchased multifamily loans that generally performed as well as or better than those of other market participants, but the Federal Housing Finance Agency (FHFA) has identified deficiencies in their credit risk management. In 2005-2008, the enterprises' serious delinquency rates (less than 1 percent) were somewhat lower than the rates on multifamily loans made by commercial banks and much lower than rates for multifamily loans funded by commercial mortgage-backed securities. FHFA, through its examination and oversight of the enterprises, identified a number of credit risk deficiencies over the past few years. For example, FHFA found deficiencies in Fannie Mae's delegated underwriting and servicing program, risk-management practices, and information systems; and Freddie Mac's management of its lower-performing assets. Both enterprises have been taking steps to address these deficiencies.

September 6, 2012

The Honorable Spencer Bachus
Chairman
Committee on Financial Services
House of Representatives

Dear Chairman Bachus:

On September 6, 2008, the Federal Housing Finance Agency (FHFA) placed Fannie Mae and Freddie Mac into conservatorship out of concern that the deteriorating financial condition of the two government-sponsored enterprises (the enterprises) threatened the stability of financial markets.[1] While the conservatorships can remain in place indefinitely as efforts are undertaken to stabilize the enterprises and restore confidence in financial markets, FHFA has said that the conservatorships were not intended to be permanent.

Most of the discussion about the future of the enterprises has focused on their role in supporting financing for single-family homes, but they have played a larger role in providing financing for multifamily properties (those with five or more units) since the financial crisis of 2007.

Congress established Fannie Mae and Freddie Mac in 1968 and 1989, respectively, as for-profit, shareholder-owned corporations. [2] They share a primary mission that has been to stabilize and assist the U.S. secondary mortgage market and facilitate the flow of mortgage credit.

To accomplish this goal, the enterprises issued debt and stock and used the proceeds to purchase conventional mortgages that met their underwriting standards from primary mortgage lenders such as banks or savings and loan associations (thrifts).[3]

In turn, banks and thrifts used the proceeds to originate additional mortgages. The enterprises purchased mortgages that they held in their portfolios or packaged into mortgage-backed securities (MBS), which were sold to investors in the secondary mortgage market.[4] In exchange for a fee (the guarantee fee), the enterprises guaranteed the timely payment of interest and principal on MBS that they issued.

Both enterprises are required to provide assistance to the secondary mortgage markets that includes purchases of mortgages that serve low- and moderate-income families. In 1992, Congress required the enterprises to meet numeric goals for the purchase of single- and multifamily conventional mortgages that serve targeted groups. Through 2008, the Department of Housing and Urban Development (HUD) set the goals for each year; FHFA currently does so.[5]

Congress and the Executive Branch will face difficult decisions on how to restructure the enterprises and promote housing opportunities while limiting risks to taxpayers and the stability of financial markets. In this context, you requested that we provide information on the history and performance of the enterprises' multifamily activities.

Specifically, this report discusses (1) how the enterprises' multifamily loan activities, products, and loan performance have changed over time, (2) the enterprises' role in the multifamily housing financing marketplace and the extent to which they have met their affordable housing goals, and (3) how the enterprises' credit standards and delinquency rates compare with those of other mortgage capital sources and how they have managed credit risk associated with their multifamily housing activities.

To describe how the enterprises' multifamily loan activities, products, and performance have changed, we analyzed loan-level data from Fannie Mae and Freddie Mac from 1994 (the earliest year for which data were available) through 2011.

For example, we analyzed the following for each enterprise:

- loans that were held in portfolio and loans that were securitized;
- loan purchases broken down by property and loan size, metropolitan area, and period of the loan;
- maturity expectations for loans purchased; and
- loan performance, including an analysis of annual serious delinquency rates.

We also analyzed aggregated data on real estate-owned, net income, net charge-offs (debts an entity is unlikely to collect), and guarantee fees. To assess data reliability, we interviewed Fannie Mae and Freddie Mac representatives about how they collected data and helped ensure data integrity and reviewed internal reports on data reliability. We also compared selected enterprise data with information in public filings. In addition, we conducted reasonableness checks on the data to identify any missing, erroneous, or outlying figures. We determined that the data were sufficiently reliable for our purposes.

To determine what is known about the enterprises' role in the overall multifamily marketplace, we reviewed reports and studies on how the enterprises helped support the market. To show how the enterprises' market share changed over the last 7 years, we analyzed flow of funds data from the Board of Governors of the Federal Reserve System (Federal Reserve) and market share data from the Mortgage Bankers Association (MBA). We met with lender, commercial real estate, and life insurance trade associations; affordable housing advocacy groups; industry researchers; and representatives from FHFA, Fannie Mae, and Freddie Mac to obtain their views on the enterprises' role.

To report on the extent to which the enterprises met affordable housing goals, we used HUD data on annual goal performance in 1993 through 2000, and analyzed data on goal performance in Annual Housing Activity Reports (activity report) provided by FHFA for 2001 through 2009. To determine the extent to which the enterprises' multifamily activities contributed to the achievement of specific goals, we calculated multifamily purchases as a percentage of total mortgage purchases under each goal using data from the activity reports.[6]

To assess the reliability of these data, we interviewed FHFA officials and representatives at Fannie Mae and Freddie Mac about how they collected and helped ensure the integrity of the information, and reviewed internal reports. We determined that the data were sufficiently reliable for our purposes.

To compare the enterprises' credit standards and delinquency rates with those of major mortgage capital sources, we analyzed loan-level data on the enterprises' loan-to-value (LTV) and debt-service coverage ratios and delinquency rates. We compared these ratios and delinquency rates with those of selected market players, including life insurance companies and commercial mortgage-backed securities (CMBS) lenders.

We interviewed officials from HUD's Federal Housing Administration (FHA), the Department of Agriculture's Rural Housing Service (RHS), the National Council of State Housing Agencies (NCSHA), the National Association of Affordable Housing Lenders, the Commercial Real Estate Finance Council, and the American Council of Life Insurers (ACLI) to obtain information on the key credit standards generally used by institutions they represent and their loan performance.

To determine the extent to which the enterprises shared risk with FHA and RHS, we obtained data on the number of loans in risk-sharing programs. We also reviewed documents describing the programs and interviewed officials from Fannie Mae, Freddie Mac, FHA, and RHS. To describe how the enterprises managed credit risk associated with their multifamily activities, we reviewed FHFA's examination reports and Office of Federal Housing Enterprise Oversight (OFHEO) and FHFA annual reports to Congress, which summarize credit risk issues identified during annual examinations of the enterprises.[7]

To describe how the enterprises have addressed or will address these issues, we reviewed the enterprises' formal responses to FHFA's examination reports and any subsequent FHFA responses. Because FHFA's examination reports and the enterprises' responses to them are confidential, we limited our discussions of them to a summary. We also made revisions based on concerns FHFA raised with our original language summarizing supervisory concerns expressed in examination reports.

We conducted this performance audit from November 2011 to September 2012 in accordance with generally accepted government auditing standards. Those standards require that we plan and perform the audit to obtain sufficient, appropriate evidence to provide a reasonable basis for our findings and conclusions based on our audit objectives.

We believe that the evidence obtained provides a reasonable basis for our findings and conclusions based on our audit objectives. Appendix I contains additional information on our scope and methodology.

BACKGROUND

The multifamily housing finance market has three principal participants: (1) primary lenders, which originate mortgage loans; (2) secondary market institutions, which purchase mortgage loans from primary lenders; and (3) investors in securities issued by secondary market institutions that are backed by mortgage loans.[8] All three participants contribute to the flow of funds to the multifamily borrower. Lenders originate mortgages, which they may either retain as an income-earning asset (an approach called portfolio lending) or sell to a secondary market institution. The sale of these mortgages provides the lender with funds to make additional loans. A secondary market institution, in turn, purchases a mortgage and may retain it as a portfolio asset or use the individual loan or a pool of loans as collateral for a security. Investors then buy these securities from a lender or secondary market institution.

Multifamily mortgages differ from single-family mortgages in several ways. A multifamily property is a cash-generating asset, with rental income used to pay the multifamily mortgage, while single-family properties are not generally cash-generating assets. Many single-family mortgages are 30-year, fully amortizing mortgages, while most multifamily loans have terms of 5, 7, or 10 years with a balloon payment due at maturity. [9] Most multifamily loans also include protection for the investor against borrower prepayment (using a prepayment premium or other limitation on prepayment), while single-family loans generally do not. In addition, multifamily mortgages have different risk characteristics. For example, it is harder to predict credit risk for multifamily mortgages than for single-family mortgages. Finally, securitizing multifamily loans (that is, packaging them into mortgage pools to support MBS) is more challenging because they are not as standardized as single-family loans. For example, the multifamily loan pools that back MBS have varied loan terms while single-family securities have historically been backed by 15- year and 30-year mortgages.

Fannie Mae and Freddie Mac were established to provide liquidity, stability, and affordability in the secondary market for both single- and multifamily mortgages. Their charters do not allow them to operate in the primary mortgage market by originating loans or lending money directly to consumers. Rather, they purchase mortgages that meet their underwriting standards from primary mortgage lenders, such as banks or thrifts, and either hold the mortgages in their portfolios or package them into MBS. Multifamily loans make up a small part of the enterprises' total loan purchases. According to FHFA's 2011 Annual Report to Congress, the enterprises purchased single-family mortgages with an unpaid principal balance of $879.0 billion and multifamily mortgages totaling $44.6 billion in 2011.

According to a 1998 article, Fannie Mae and Freddie Mac both entered the conventional multifamily loan market in 1983 and were experiencing significant losses by 1991.[10] For example, the article stated that in 1991, Fannie Mae's multifamily loans were 5.7 percent of all its loans, but multifamily charge-offs were 30.2 percent of its total charge-offs.[11] Freddie Mac's 1991 losses were even greater. According to the article, its multifamily loans were 2.6 percent of all loans, but multifamily charge-offs were 51.4 percent of its total charge-offs.[12] Due to these losses, Freddie Mac exited the multifamily market for 3 years starting in 1991.[13] The same article noted that boom-and-bust cycles are common in the multifamily housing market due to the relative ease of entry into the industry. During periods of strong performance, new apartment supply increases, which leads to overexpansion and high vacancy rates.

According to the authors, such a cycle contributed to the enterprises' losses in the late 1980s.

Fannie Mae currently participates in the multifamily mortgage finance market primarily through its Delegated Underwriting and Servicing (DUS®) program. Under this program, which was initiated in 1988, Fannie Mae approves lenders and delegates to them the authority to underwrite, close, and sell loans to the enterprise without its prior review.[14]

In exchange for granting this authority, DUS lenders share the risk of loss with Fannie Mae. The most common loss-sharing structures are standard DUS loss sharing and pari passu. The standard model has a tiered loss system, generally with the maximum lender loss capped at the first 20 percent of the original loan amount. Under the pari passu model, lenders share all losses on a pro rata basis with Fannie Mae (the lender assumes one-third of the loss and Fannie Mae two-thirds).

A small portion of Fannie Mae's multifamily business comprises non-DUS deliveries, which typically are small balance loans or pools of seasoned loans (loans that have typically been in a financial institution's portfolio for at least 1 year and have a satisfactory repayment record). In 1994, Fannie Mae began securitizing DUS loans by creating DUS MBS, each of which is backed by a Fannie Mae guarantee to the investor of principal and interest. Typically, each DUS MBS pool contains one DUS loan, but can incorporate multiple DUS loans.

Freddie Mac participates in the multifamily market by underwriting all of the loans it purchases.[15] It purchases loans from a network of approved lenders, but completes the underwriting and credit reviews in-house. Freddie Mac also conducts negotiated transactions or purchases of seasoned loans. For a majority of its business, Freddie Mac sells a significant amount of multifamily credit risk, as defined by expected losses, to investors by issuing securities backed by its mortgages. In general, these securities, known as K-deals, are backed by pools of newly originated mortgages underwritten by Freddie Mac.[16]

Loss-sharing arrangements such as Fannie Mae's DUS program and Freddie Mac's K-deal program do not exist in either enterprise's single-family business.

In addition to Fannie Mae and Freddie Mac, the following entities participate in the multifamily housing financing marketplace:

- Life insurance companies originate and hold in portfolio multifamily mortgages.
- CMBS lenders originate multifamily loans that are packaged into CMBS, which are MBS backed by commercial rather than residential properties. Commercial properties include multifamily housing as well as retail, office, and industrial space.
- Commercial banks and thrifts originate commercial and industrial loans, including loans secured by multifamily properties. They may retain these loans in their portfolios or sell them to the enterprises or other secondary market investors.
- FHA insures multifamily loans originated by FHA-approved lenders for the construction, substantial rehabilitation, and acquisition and refinancing of apartments.
- RHS has a guaranteed loan program for rural multifamily housing.
- State and local housing finance agencies (HFA) are state or locally chartered authorities established to help meet the affordable housing needs of the residents of their states or localities. HFAs sell tax-exempt housing bonds, commonly known as Multifamily Housing Bonds, to investors to finance multifamily housing production.

Loan consortiums—which are organized by a group of commercial banks and savings institutions in a local housing market or at the state level to provide multifamily affordable construction and mortgage loans—are primary lenders for multifamily housing with less than 50 units.

The Enterprises' Multifamily Loan Activities Generally Increased and Delinquencies Remained Low

From 1994 through 2011, the multifamily loan activities of Fannie Mae and Freddie Mac generally increased, while delinquency rates remained relatively low. During this period, the number of loans they purchased spiked in some years to meet goals for financing affordable housing. Fannie Mae has held a lower percentage of its loans in portfolio than Freddie Mac, but both enterprises have increased securitization activities in recent years partly in response to a mandate from the Department of the Treasury (Treasury) to reduce retained portfolios.[17] Serious delinquency rates for the enterprises' multifamily loans were generally less than 1 percent from 1994 through 2011, but the unpaid principal balance on seriously delinquent loans rose considerably starting in 2008. For all of the analyses of Fannie Mae and Freddie Mac's purchases, we adjusted the dollar amounts for inflation to 2012 dollars. As a result, the numbers we present are unlikely to correspond to similar numbers previously reported by the enterprises in their public disclosures.

Multifamily Loan Purchases Peaked in Recent Years, with Some Fluctuation Tied to Housing Goals

From 1994 through 2011, the enterprises' multifamily loan activities generally increased. As shown in figure 1, the enterprises' annual purchases of multifamily loans (in terms of unpaid principal balances) dramatically increased starting in 2000, peaked in 2007 and 2008, and generally declined in the years following.[18] Fannie Mae's purchases ranged from $6.3 billion in 1994 to $49.8 billion in 2007. Freddie Mac's purchases ranged from $885.5 million in 1994 to $25.5 billion in 2008. The enterprises' annual loan purchases increased dramatically in 2007 and 2008 as other participants exited the market during the financial crisis.

The enterprises' multifamily activities (by number of loans acquired) varied over the period we reviewed, in some cases because the enterprises purchased additional loans to meet affordable housing goals. For example, Fannie Mae acquired a large number of loans in 2003 and 2007, and Freddie Mac in 2003. According to Fannie Mae officials, the majority of these acquisitions were pools of seasoned multifamily loans purchased through negotiated transactions to meet affordable housing goals for the purchase of mortgages that served targeted groups such as low- and moderate-income households. Freddie Mac officials offered a similar explanation for the increase in their 2003 purchases. From 2003 through 2007, affordable housing goals were set as the percentage of the enterprises' total (single-family and multifamily) mortgage purchases. Increased activity in the single-family financing market in 2003 and 2007 (that is, more people buying and refinancing homes) meant that the enterprise needed to acquire more mortgages to meet affordable housing goals. As discussed in more detail later in this report, multifamily mortgages had a disproportionate importance for the housing goals because most multifamily housing serves targeted groups.

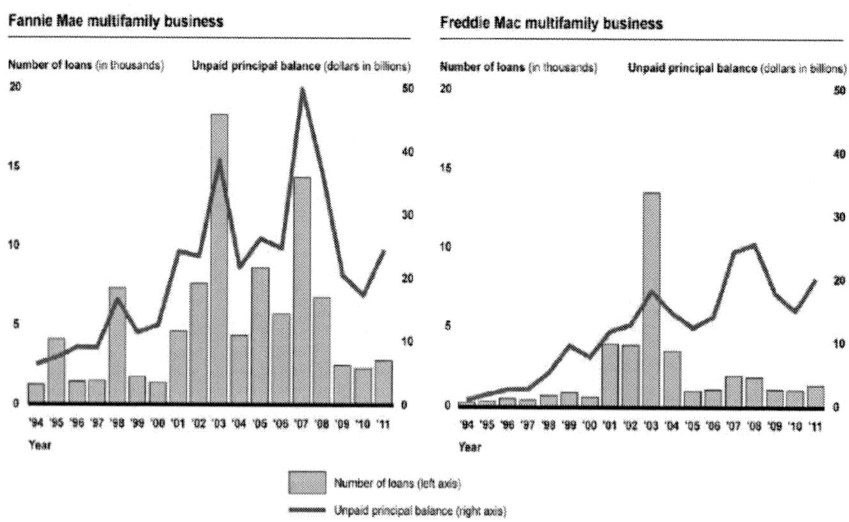

Source: GAO analysis of Fannie Mae and Freddie Mac data.
Note: All dollar figures are in 2012 dollars.

Figure 1. Enterprises' Annual Multifamily Loan Purchases by Number of Loans and Unpaid Principal Balance, 1994-2011.

Fannie Mae Retained a Lower Percentage of Multifamily Loans Than Freddie Mac

From 1994 through 2011, Fannie Mae retained a lower percentage of its annual multifamily loan purchases in portfolio at acquisition than Freddie Mac (see fig. 2).[19] From 1994 through 2003, the majority of Fannie Mae's multifamily loan purchases were packaged into MBS. The percentage of unpaid principal balance associated with these MBS ranged from 53 percent ($3.3 billion) in 1994 to 86 percent ($14.3 billion) in 1998. From 2004 through 2008, this trend reversed, with the majority of the unpaid principal balance of Fannie Mae's loan acquisitions being held in portfolio as whole loans. The percentages held in portfolio ranged from 50 percent ($10.8 billion) in 2004 to 82 percent ($41 billion) in 2007. Following the conservatorship, the majority of Fannie Mae's loan purchases were again packaged into MBS, with the 2011 data showing that 98.6 percent ($24.1 billion) of the unpaid principal balance of multifamily loans Fannie Mae acquired that year was securitized.

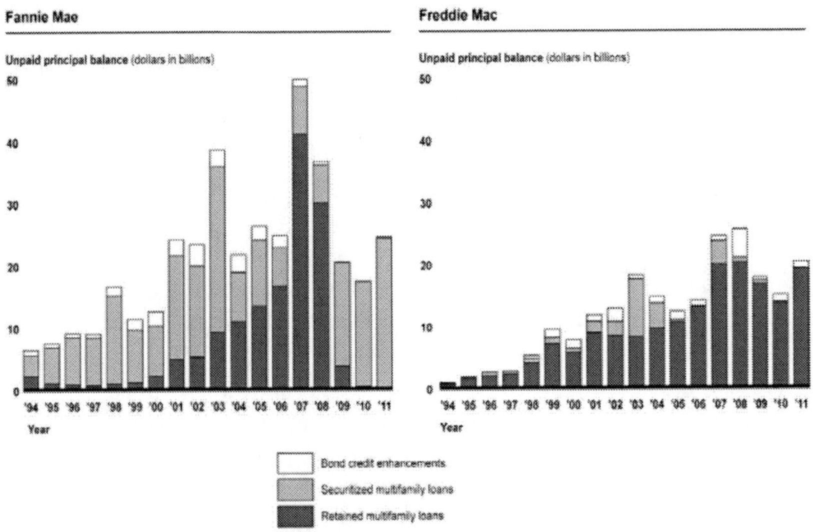

Source: GAO analysis of Fannie Mae and Freddie Mac data.

Note: All dollar figures are in 2012 dollars. Starting in 2008, Freddie Mac's retained multifamily loans were comprised of loans held for investment and loans held for sale. According to Freddie Mac officials, loans held for investment were those it planned to hold in its portfolio until maturity. Loans held for sale were those that Freddie Mac initially held in its portfolio but planned to include in a K-deal (that is, securitize) at a future time. (Table 1 shows the unpaid principal balance of loans held for investment and loans held for sale from 2008 through 2011.) This figure categorizes loans for 1994 through 2011 based on whether they were retained in portfolio or securitized at acquisition.

Figure 2. Enterprises' Annual Volume of Retained Multifamily Loans, Securitized Multifamily Loans, and Multifamily Bond Credit Enhancements, 1994-2011.

As previously discussed, Treasury required the enterprises to reduce their retained portfolios each year (starting in 2010) as a condition of agreements providing financial support.

Prior to 2008, the majority of Freddie Mac's multifamily business (in terms of unpaid principal balance) remained in its retained portfolio. Retained loans represented the majority of Freddie Mac's multifamily business in every year from 1994 through 2007 except 2003. The percentage of unpaid principal balance retained ranged from 65 percent ($8.3 billion) in 2002 to 93 percent ($13 billion) in 2006. In 2003, the percentage of unpaid principal balance securitized was 51 percent ($9.3 billion), while the percentage retained was 45 percent ($8.1 billion). Bond credit enhancements constituted the remainder (4 percent) of its multifamily business in 2003.

Separate and apart from the portfolio reduction requirement in the preferred stock purchase agreement, Freddie Mac started a new program in 2008, which it called K-certificates or K-deals, to securitize its loans and sell a significant portion of the credit risk associated with the loans.[20] With the start of the K-deal program, Freddie Mac began categorizing multifamily loans it held in portfolio at acquisition as loans held for investment and loans held for sale.

According to Freddie Mac officials, loans held for investment were those it planned to hold in its portfolio until maturity. Loans held for sale were those that Freddie Mac initially held in its portfolio but planned to include in a K-deal (that is, securitize) at a future time. According to officials, loans held for sale were almost always securitized. Table 1 shows the unpaid principal balance of loans held for investment and loans held for sale from 2008 through 2011. Loans held for sale had become the predominant loan type by 2010.

Table 1. Unpaid Principal Balance of Multifamily Loans That Freddie Mac Held for Investment and Held for Sale, 2008-2011

Acquisition year	Unpaid principal balance of loans held for investment (dollars in millions)	Unpaid principal balance of loans held for sale (dollars in millions)
2008	$19,600	$497
2009	11,840	4,826
2010	2,988	10,598
2011	2,391	16,642

Source: GAO analysis of Freddie Mac data.

Note: All dollar figures are in 2012 dollars.

The enterprises may hold their own MBS in their retained portfolio. Fannie Mae officials indicated that MBS it purchased were typically either resold in their original state or resecuritized with the purpose of making them a more suitable investment for a broader range of participants. They noted that their goal was to hold MBS purchases temporarily and to operate in a manner that is consistent with the FHFA directive to reduce the size of the retained mortgage portfolio. Data on Fannie Mae's multifamily MBS portfolio balance for 2010 through 2011 showed that its portfolio grew from $9.5 billion at the beginning of 2010 to $28.3 billion at the end of 2011. The majority of this growth was due to the securitization of multifamily whole loans previously held in their portfolio with an unpaid principal balance of $18.7 billion. Fannie Mae started this initiative in the fourth quarter of 2010 in response to Treasury's requirement to reduce its retained portfolio. Its sales and purchases of multifamily MBS in the secondary market were about the same. For example, during 2011 it purchased and sold MBS totaling about $11 billion. Data on Freddie Mac's purchases of its own MBS in 2010 and 2011 show that the enterprise purchased $382 million and $472 million, respectively. These amounts were about 4 percent of the MBS issued each year.

Enterprises Generally Financed Large Multifamily Properties in Large Metropolitan Areas

Size of Multifamily Properties Financed

The majority of Fannie Mae and Freddie Mac's purchases of multifamily loans, as measured by unpaid principal balance, were for properties with more than 50 units (see fig. 3). For example, from 1994 through 2011, Fannie Mae acquired $292.0 billion of multifamily loans for properties with more than 50 units, compared to $56.2 billion of loans for properties with 5 to 50 units. Similarly, Freddie Mac acquired $199.1 billion of multifamily loans for properties with more than 50 units, compared to $15.4 billion of loans for properties with 5 to 50 units. While the majority of the unpaid principal balance was on loans for properties with more than 50 units, the enterprises acquired more loans for properties with 5 to 50 units over this period. For example, from 1994 through 2011 Fannie Mae purchased 62,353 multifamily loans for properties with 5 to 50 units and 33,178 loans for properties with more than 50 units. Similarly, Freddie Mac purchased 20,900 multifamily loans for properties with 5 to 50 units and 15,817 loans for properties with more than 50 units.

Both enterprises purchased the highest number of loans for properties with 5 to 50 units in 2003. According to FHFA officials, the enterprises purchased a large number of loans for smaller properties that year because they received "bonus points" toward meeting their affordable housing goals when they purchased these mortgages.21 Fannie Mae also purchased a large number of loans for properties with 5 to 50 units in 2007. As noted previously, these purchases helped them meet their affordable housing goals that year although the bonus points were no longer in effect.

Freddie Mac purchased the vast majority of its loans for smaller properties in 2001 through 2003, when the bonus points were in effect. Since 2005, Freddie Mac has purchased very few multifamily loans for smaller properties. According to Freddie Mac officials, the enterprise is not currently active in the small multifamily loan market in part because of the credit characteristics of these loans. While they are considered by definition to be "multifamily" properties because they have five or more units, these transactions generally need to be underwritten more similarly to single-family loans.

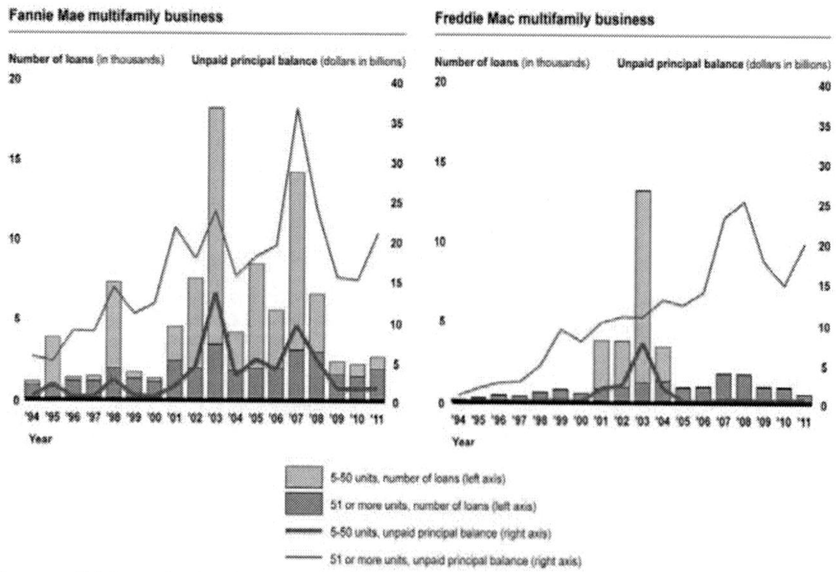

Source: GAO analysis of Fannie Mae and Freddie Mac data.
Note: All dollar figures are in 2012 dollars.

Figure 3. Enterprises' Multifamily Loan Purchases by Unit Size of Properties, 1994-2011.

Freddie Mac officials noted that because the cost of underwriting is essentially the same for loans on larger and smaller properties, purchasing loans on small income properties on an individual loan basis is less cost-effective than the purchase of individual loans on larger properties. We discuss the enterprises' role in this market segment in more detail later in this report.

Size of Multifamily Loans at Acquisition

The majority of the multifamily loans that the enterprises purchased, as measured by unpaid principal balances, were for loans with balances at acquisition of $5 million to less than $50 million (see fig. 4). From 1994 through 2011, Fannie Mae purchased $203.5 billion of multifamily loans in this category, while Freddie Mac purchased $155.1 billion of multifamily loans of this size.

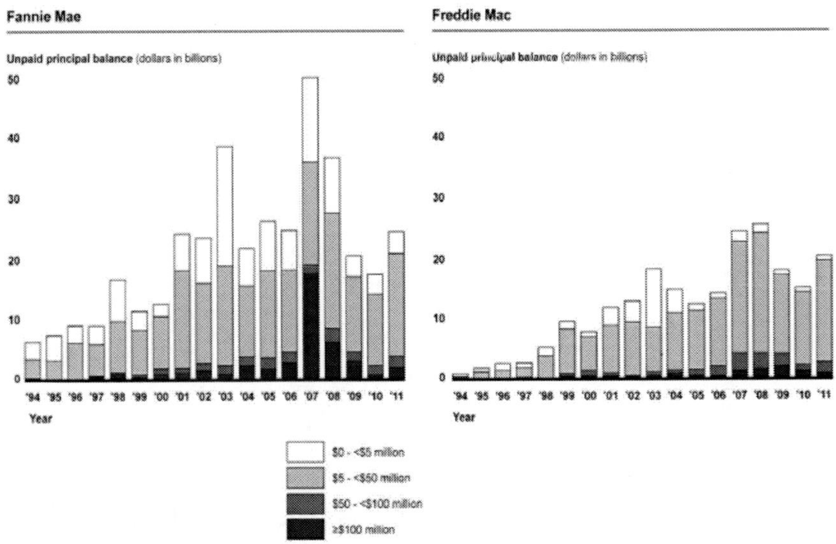

Source: GAO analysis of Fannie Mae and Freddie Mac data.
Note: All dollar figures are in 2012 dollars.

Figure 4. Enterprises' Annual Multifamily Loan Purchases by Loan Size at Acquisition, 1994-2011.

While the majority of the unpaid principal balance was on multifamily loans with balances at acquisition of $5 million to less than $50 million, the enterprises acquired more multifamily loans with balances at acquisition of less than $5 million. For example, from 1994 through 2011 Fannie Mae purchased 81,156 multifamily loans with balances at acquisition of less than $5 million and 15,425 multifamily loans with larger loan balances. Similarly, Freddie Mac purchased 26,944 multifamily loans with balances at acquisition of less than $5 million and 10,202 multifamily loans with larger loan balances.

Geographic Location of Multifamily Properties Financed

The majority of the multifamily loans that the enterprises purchased were loans for properties in the largest metropolitan areas. We used 2010 U.S. Census Bureau data to identify the 25 largest metropolitan statistical areas (MSA) by population.[22]

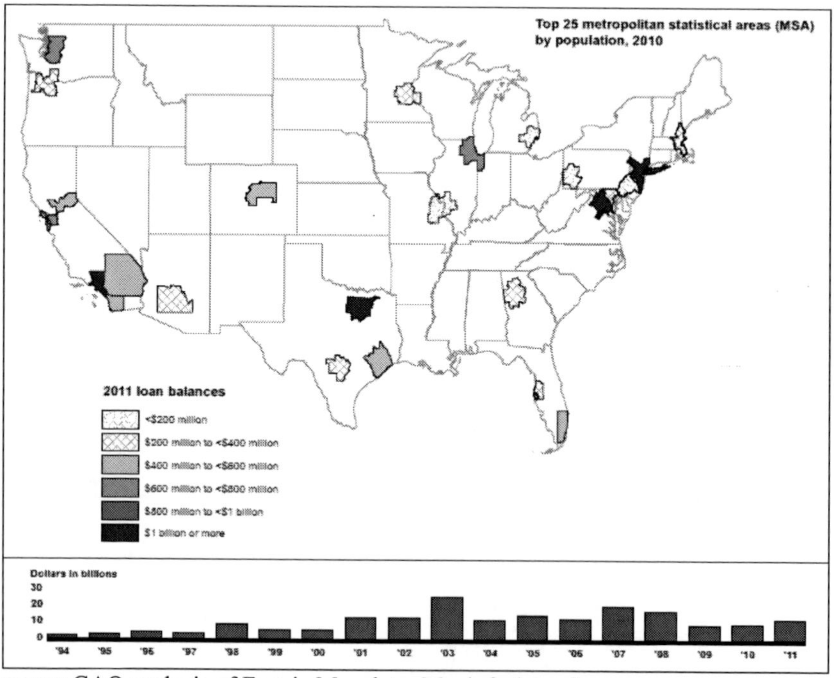

Sources: GAO analysis of Fannie Mae data; Mapinfo (maps).

Note: All dollar figures are in 2012 dollars. We included only those purchases where a single loan was associated with a single property. As discussed later in this report, Fannie Mae offers financing options that can result in one loan for multiple properties, multiple loans for multiple properties, or multiple loans for one property.

Figure 5. Fannie Mae's Annual Purchases of Multifamily Loans in 25 Largest Metropolitan Areas, 1994-2011.

Data from the 2010 American Community Survey show that 56.3 percent of the nation's multifamily housing was located in these 25 MSAs. For Fannie Mae, 69 percent of the unpaid principal balance of multifamily loans it purchased from 1994 through 2011 was for properties located in these 25 MSAs (see figure 5). Further, from 1994 through 2011, the loans that Freddie Mac purchased for properties in the 25 largest MSAs constituted 68 percent of its unpaid principal balance (see fig. 6). For information on both enterprises' purchases by metropolitan area and state, see appendixes II and III, respectively.

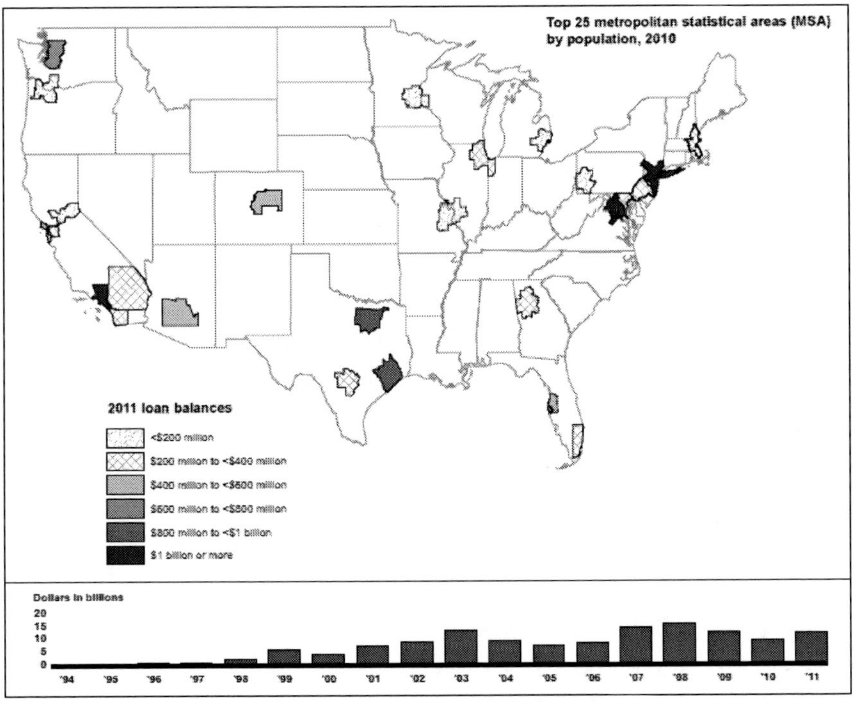

Sources: GAO analysis of Freddie Mac data; Mapinfo (maps).
Note: All dollar figures are in 2012 dollars.

Figure 6. Freddie Mac's Annual Purchases of Multifamily Loans in 25 Largest Metropolitan Areas, 1994-2011.

Multifamily Loan Terms

In terms of unpaid principal balance, over half of the multifamily loans that Fannie Mae purchased and almost half of the multifamily loans that Freddie Mac purchased from 1994 through 2011 were loans with terms of 60,

84, and 120 months (5, 7, and 10 years). This is in contrast to single-family mortgages purchased by the enterprises, many of which were 30- year mortgages.

Figure 7 shows that with some exceptions the enterprises annually purchased more multifamily loans with terms of 120 months than any other category. The exceptions were 1994-1995 and 2003 for Fannie Mae and 1994 and 2001-2007 for Freddie Mac. During these years, loans with terms longer than 120 months generally constituted the largest category. According to Fannie Mae officials, the enterprise has periodically purchased pools of seasoned loans with loan terms greater than 120 months.

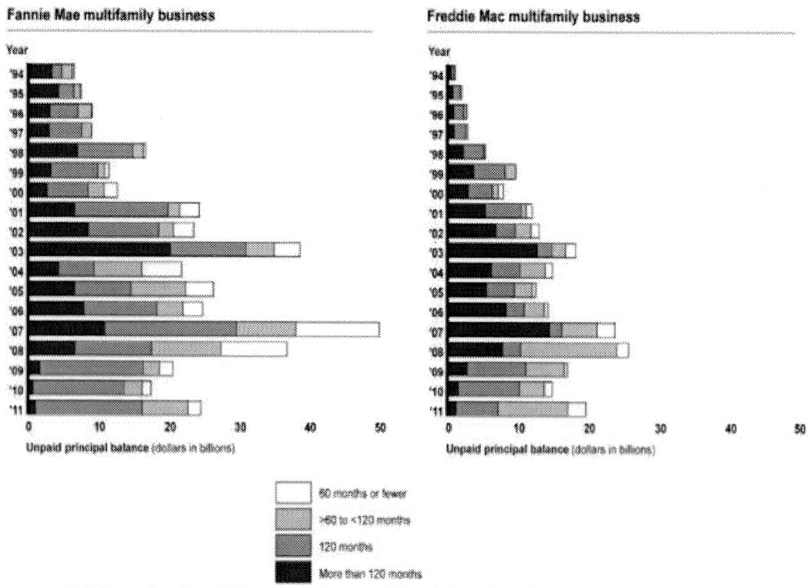

Source: GAO analysis of Fannie Mae and Freddie Mac data.
Note: All dollar figures are in 2012 dollars.

Figure 7. Fannie Mae and Freddie Mac Multifamily Loan Terms, 1994-2011.

Multifamily Asset Class

The enterprises acquired multifamily loans for a variety of asset classes—traditional rental, student, senior, manufactured, and cooperative housing—but the majority of the multifamily properties that they financed from 1994 through 2011 were traditional rental properties.[23] As shown in figure 8, 87.7 percent of Fannie Mae's multifamily mortgage purchases during this period and 91.6 percent of Freddie Mac's multifamily mortgage purchases were loans for traditional rental housing.[24] The enterprises explained this occurred because the majority of the multifamily mortgage market is concentrated in traditional rental housing.

Type of Interest Rate for Multifamily Loans

While the vast majority of the multifamily loans that the enterprises purchased from 1994 through 2011 were fixed-rate loans, they also acquired a large number of adjustable-rate mortgages (ARM) in 2003 that coincided with the acquisition of seasoned loans to meet affordable housing goals described earlier (see fig. 9). From 1994 through 2011, Fannie Mae purchased $291.8 billion in fixed-rate mortgages and $87 billion in ARMs, and Freddie Mac purchased $165.1 billion in fixed-rate mortgages and $48.6 billion in ARMs. During this period, yearly fixed-rate purchases typically represented 67 percent or more of all multifamily mortgage purchases (in terms of unpaid principal balances). However, in 2003 Fannie Mae's purchases of fixed-rate mortgages fell to 54 percent of all multifamily purchases and Freddie Mac's to 47 percent.

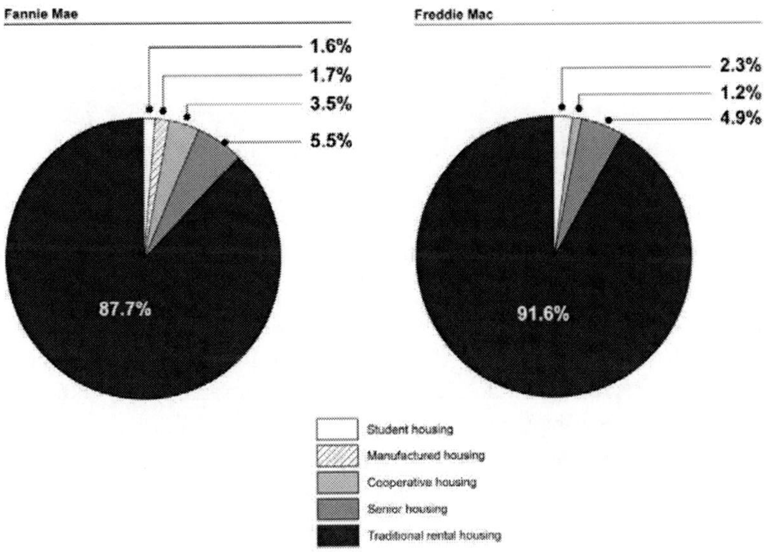

Source: GAO analysis of Fannie Mae and Freddie Mac data.

Note: Manufactured housing is not reflected on the Freddie Mac pie chart because it only purchased two of these loans from 1994 through 2011.

Figure 8. Enterprises' Multifamily Loan Purchases by Asset Class, 1994-2011.

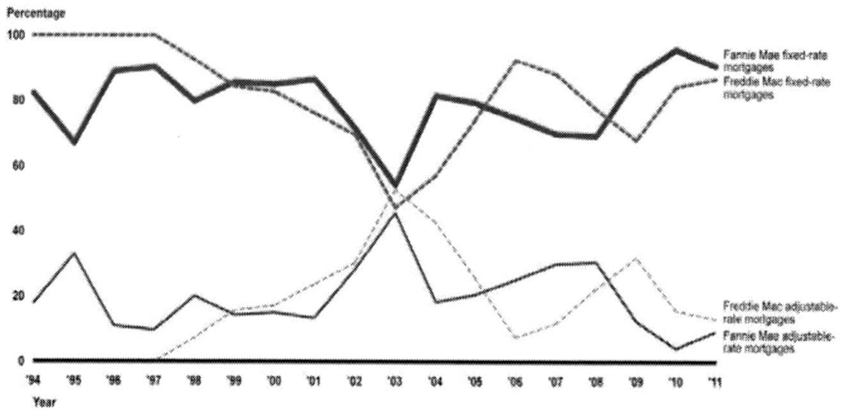

Source: GAO analysis of Fannie Mae and Freddie Mac data.

Note: During the first 4 years we analyzed, Freddie Mac purchased no ARM multifamily loans.

Figure 9. Enterprises' Annual Multifamily Loan Purchases by Interest Rate Type, 1994-2011.

According to Fannie Mae officials, multifamily borrowers typically selected ARMs when they wanted to maintain greater prepayment flexibility and when the interest rate environment favored ARMs. According to Freddie Mac officials, the majority of ARMs that the enterprise has acquired are related to the affordable business described earlier in the report.

Structured Multifamily Finance and Fannie Mae's DUS Program

The enterprises exhibited some differences in their approaches to purchasing multifamily loans from 1994 through 2011. For example, both enterprises provided a structuring option that allowed a borrower to arrange financing terms for a group of loans and properties, but Fannie Mae much more so than Freddie Mac.25 At Fannie Mae, these transactions could involve multiple properties financed by one loan, multiple properties financed by multiple loans, or one property financed by multiple loans. For certain transactions, the number of loans and properties can change over time as the borrower sells certain properties and acquires new ones, and needs new infusions of capital to finance these acquisitions. At Freddie Mac, such transactions could involve multiple properties financed by one loan or one property financed by multiple loans. Although most of Fannie Mae's multifamily purchases continued to involve one property financed by one loan, it started engaging in these transactions in a significant way in the early 2000s (see fig. 10). By 2007, 16 percent ($8 billion) of Fannie Mae's loan acquisitions occurred within transactions featuring multiple loans for multiple properties. Also in 2007, 20 percent ($10 billion) of Fannie Mae's loan acquisitions occurred within transactions featuring one loan for multiple properties. In contrast, from 1994 through 2011 Freddie Mac's transactions involving multiple loans or multiple properties represented about 0.1 percent of the loans it purchased and about 1 percent of its unpaid principal balance.

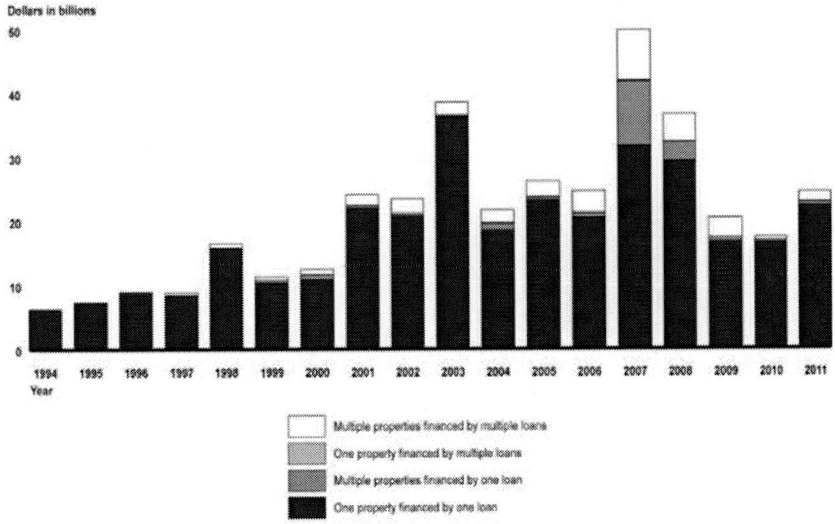

Source: GAO analysis of Fannie Mae data.
Note: All dollar figures are in 2012 dollars.

Figure 10. Fannie Mae's Use of Various Multifamily Structuring Options.

In contrast to Freddie Mac, which underwrites all the loans it purchases, Fannie Mae delegates the majority of its underwriting (based on unpaid principal balance) through its DUS program. From 1994 through 2011, loans purchased under the DUS program represented the majority of Fannie Mae's multifamily loan purchases in terms of unpaid principal balance for every year except 1994, 1995, 2003, and 2007 (see fig. 11, left). A smaller portion of Fannie Mae's multifamily business comprised non-DUS deliveries, which typically were small balance loans or pools of seasoned loans.

However, based on total loan counts, non-DUS loans constituted the majority of multifamily loans in 10 of the 18 years we reviewed (see fig. 11, right). In addition, some of the years in which non-DUS loans were the majority were the same years in which the enterprises acquired many more multifamily loans to meet housing goals. For example, in 2003 Fannie Mae purchased 16,322 non-DUS loans (representing $19.8 billion in unpaid principal balance) and 1,995 DUS loans (representing $18.7 billion), and in 2007 it purchased 11,819 non-DUS loans (representing $27.0 billion) and 2,552 DUS loans (representing $22.8 billion).

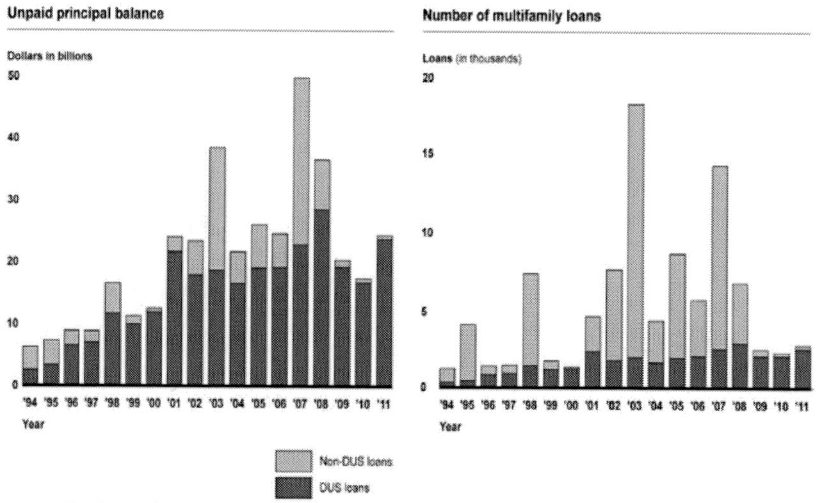

Source: GAO analysis of Fannie Mae data.
Note: All dollar figures are in 2012 dollars.

Figure 11. Fannie Mae's Annual Multifamily Loan Purchases by Type of Underwriting, 1994-2011.

Enterprises' Multifamily Serious Delinquency Rates Were Low

From 1994 through 2011, Fannie Mae and Freddie Mac's multifamily serious delinquency rates, based on unpaid principal balances, were below 1 percent with the exception of Fannie Mae in 1994 (see fig. 12).[26] However, starting in 2008 Fannie Mae's serious delinquency rates and the total unpaid principal balance of seriously delinquent loans increased. For example, in 2008 the unpaid principal balance of seriously delinquent loans was $500.9 million (0.29 percent), but rose to $1.3 billion (0.70 percent) in 2010 and dropped to $1.1 billion (0.58 percent) in 2011. Freddie Mac also saw a rise in serious delinquency rates and the unpaid principal balance of seriously delinquent loans starting in 2008. In that year, the unpaid principal balance of delinquent loans was $31.5 million (0.03 percent), but increased to $293.9 million (0.26 percent) in 2010 and dropped to $259.7 million (0.22 percent) in 2011. These increases in serious delinquency rates and seriously delinquent unpaid principal balances in 2008 through 2011 could be attributable to loans purchased in prior years.[27] However, past performance is not necessarily indicative of future performance. As the enterprises continue to purchase multifamily mortgages, the quality of such loans and economic conditions will influence delinquency rates.

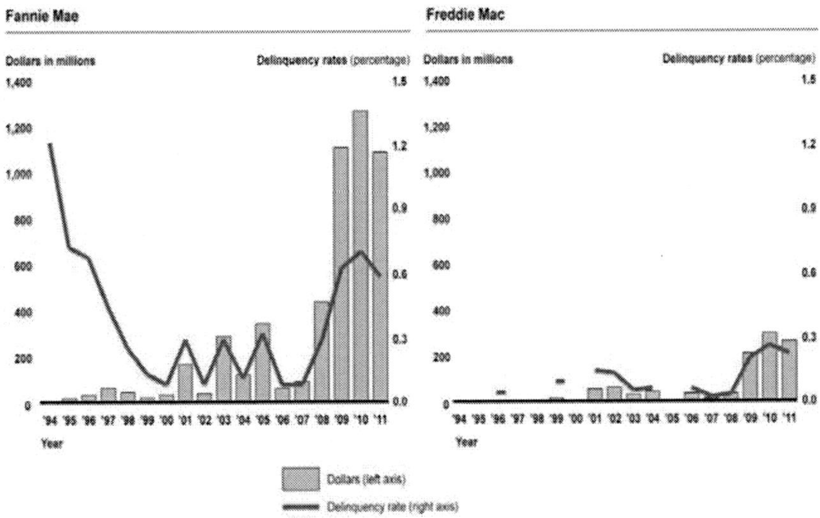

Source: GAO analysis of Fannie Mae data.

Note: For Freddie Mac, delinquency rates were 0 percent in 1994, 1995, 1997, 1998, and 2000.

Figure 12. Unpaid Principal Balances of Enterprises' Seriously Delinquent Multifamily Loans and Multifamily Portfolio Serious Delinquency Rates, 1994-2011.

Similar to delinquencies, the unpaid principal balance of Fannie Mae and Freddie Mac's multifamily loans associated with real estate-owned (REO) properties—those acquired through foreclosure—remained low overall but increased in recent years. From 2002 to 2011, Fannie Mae's unpaid principal balance on REO properties ranged from $9 million in 2002 to $1.2 billion in 2010 (see fig. 13).

Total end-of-year unpaid principal balance has increased substantially for Fannie Mae since 2007, which was the beginning of the financial crisis. After

1995, Freddie Mac's portfolio of multifamily REO (by unpaid principal balance) remained low until 2010, increasing from $52 million in 2009 to $171 million in 2010.

While the enterprises' multifamily serious delinquency rates remained low from 1994 to 2011, many of their multifamily loans will mature in the next 10 years. Specifically, a majority of the loans the enterprises currently hold are scheduled to mature by 2018. Between 2012 and 2018, 20,703 of the loans that Fannie Mae purchased (52.5 percent of its multifamily portfolio as of December 2011) are scheduled to mature. The unpaid principal balance of these loans is $108 billion, or 58.4 percent of Fannie Mae's total multifamily unpaid principal balance as of December 2011.

	Fannie Mae		Freddie Mac	
	Unpaid principal balance (dollars in millions)	Percentage of book of business	Unpaid principal balance (dollars in millions)	Percentage of book of business
1995	No data	No data	$104	1.560 %
1996	No data	No data	32	0.427
1997	No data	No data	12	0.143
1998	No data	No data	6	0.054
1999	No data	No data	1	0.006
2000	No data	No data	2	0.009
2001	No data	No data	2	0.007
2002	$9	0.01 %	1	0.003
2003	90	0.09	39	0.079
2004	151	0.13	2	0.004
2005	66	0.05	18	0.032
2006	58	0.05	10	0.018
2007	47	0.03	0	0.000
2008	129	0.07	60	0.068
2009	422	0.23	52	0.051
2010	1,222	0.65	171	0.156
2011	1,097	0.56	161	0.154

Source: Fannie Mae and Freddie Mac.

Note: Fannie Mae could not provide data before 2002 because this was prior to its restatement of earnings. Freddie Mac was not able to provide data for 1994.

Figure 13. Unpaid Principal Balances of Enterprises' Multifamily REO Property and Multifamily REO Property as a Percentage of Multifamily Book of Business, 1995-2011.

Between 2012 and 2018, 5,975 of the loans that Freddie Mac purchased (57.2 percent of its portfolio as of December 2011) are scheduled to mature.

This represents $69.7 billion, or 60.1 percent of Freddie Mac's unpaid principal balance as of December 2011.

Enterprises' Multifamily Activity Generally Was Profitable

From 2002 through 2011, Fannie Mae and Freddie Mac's multifamily business operations generally were profitable, except for losses both enterprises reported for 2008 and 2009. We reviewed three measures affecting profitability: net income, net charge-offs, and guarantee fees.[28]

Multifamily Net Income

Due to differences in the business structures of the enterprises, net income figures cannot be directly compared between enterprises.[29] Fannie Mae's multifamily business reported positive net income every year from 2002 through 2011 except for 2008 and 2009 (see fig. 14). In those years, it lost $2.2 billion and $9 billion, respectively. Fannie Mae had to write off low-income housing tax credit (LIHTC) investments, which constituted the majority of the loss reported for 2009.[30] Freddie Mac's multifamily business reported positive net income every year from 2005 to 2011 except for 2008 and 2009.

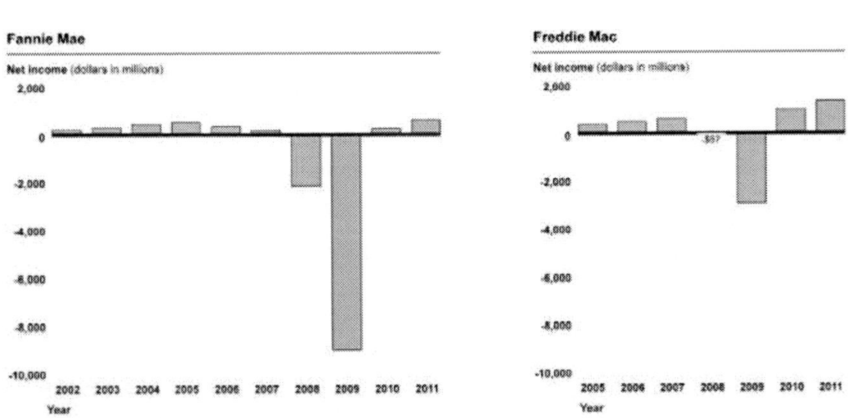

Source: Fannie Mae and Freddie Mac.

Note: Fannie Mae data were not available before 2002, and Freddie Mac data were not available before 2005.

Figure 14. Net Income Attributable to Fannie Mae and Freddie Mac's Multifamily Business, 2002-2011.

In those years, it lost $57 million and $3 billion, respectively. Similar to Fannie Mae, the loss Freddie Mac reported for 2009 was primarily due to LIHTC write-offs.

Multifamily Net Charge-offs

Net multifamily charge-offs increased in recent years, mirroring the rise in serious delinquencies shown earlier.[31] From 2002 to 2008, net charge-offs in Fannie Mae's multifamily business segment remained at or below $34 million annually (see fig. 15). Since 2008, annual net charge-offs have risen dramatically, peaking at $446 million (a loss rate of 0.61 percent) in 2010. From 2002 to 2008, annual net charge-offs in Freddie Mac's multifamily business segment remained at or below $8 million, with one year during that period resulting in a net gain. However, since 2008, annual net charge-offs have risen, including a net charge-off of $103 million (a loss rate of 0.10 percent) in 2010.

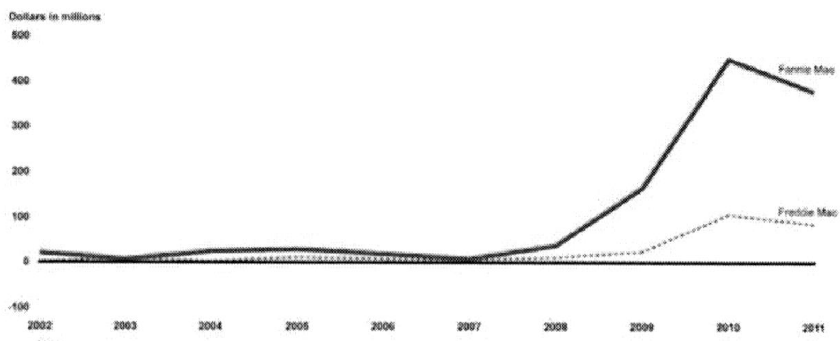

Source: Fannie Mae and Freddie Mac.

Note: Fannie Mae data were not available before 2002, and Freddie Mac data were not available before 1997.

Figure 15. Net Charge-offs Attributable to Fannie Mae and Freddie Mac's Multifamily Business, 2002-2011.

Multifamily Guarantee Fees

Multifamily guarantee fees for both enterprises grew from 2002 to 2011. Fannie Mae's guarantee fees are compensation received for assuming and managing credit risk on the mortgage loans underlying its MBS, multifamily loans held in its portfolio, and other mortgage-related securities. From 2002 through 2011, Fannie Mae's multifamily business received between $271 million and $884 million in guarantee fees annually, as shown in figure 16. Guarantee fees—which are charged to investors for guaranteeing the payment of principal and interest on multifamily mortgage-related securities and mortgages underlying multifamily housing revenue bonds—are a relatively small source of revenue for Freddie Mac. From 2002 through 2011, Freddie Mac's multifamily business received between $38 million and $127 million in guarantee fees annually.

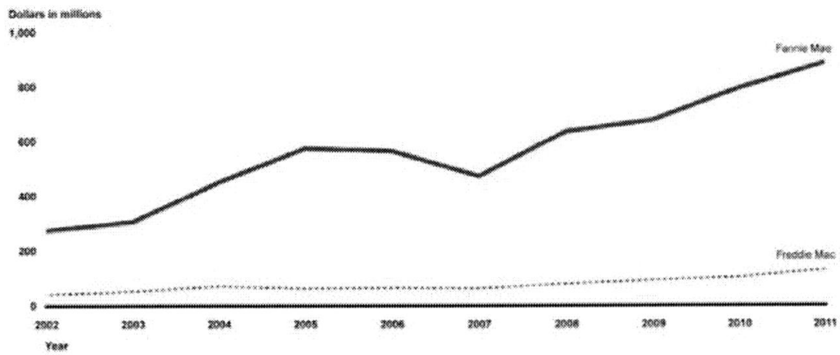

Source: Fannie Mae and Freddie Mac.

Note: Fannie Mae data were not available before 2002, and Freddie Mac data were not available before 2001.

Figure 16. Multifamily Guarantee Fees Received by Fannie Mae and Freddie Mac, 2002-2011.

According to Freddie Mac officials, the gains (or losses) on mortgages held for sale have become a bigger driver of net income than guarantee fees. Freddie Mac's total gain on loans held for securitization is represented by both the gains it receives while the loans are held in portfolio awaiting securitization and gains it receives upon securitizing the loans. With the expansion of its securitization business, or K-deal program, combined gains on the sale of mortgages have increased from $14 million in 2008 to $300 million in 2011.

Enterprises Increased Their Multifamily Market Share and Generally Met Affordable Housing Goals

Fannie Mae and Freddie Mac have played an increasingly large role in the multifamily marketplace since the beginning of the financial crisis in 2007, as evidenced by the increase in their market share. Although empirical research on the enterprises' role in multifamily housing financing is limited, the literature we reviewed generally stated that the enterprises have provided liquidity and market stability. The enterprises met their affordable housing goals in most years, with multifamily activities greatly contributing to their fulfillment.

Enterprises' Multifamily Market Share Has Grown Since the Financial Crisis

Although the enterprises historically have played a smaller role in financing multifamily housing than single-family housing, their role in the multifamily housing financing marketplace has grown since the financial crisis began in 2007, as evidenced by the increase in their market share. We relied on two sources of data on market share in the multifamily housing financing marketplace from 2005 through 2011: (1) data from the Federal Reserve on all multifamily mortgage debt outstanding and (2) MBA data on sources of financing for mortgages originated in a given year. Our analysis of Federal Reserve data shows that as of the end of 2011, the enterprises held or guaranteed almost 34 percent of the outstanding multifamily mortgage debt compared to about 24 percent in 2005 (see fig. 17).

According to MBA data on the financing of loans by investor type, the enterprises financed less than 30 percent of annual multifamily loans originated before 2008 (see fig. 18). Their share of the multifamily market increased to 86 percent in 2009, but decreased to about 57 percent in 2011 as other participants reentered the market. These data are based on MBA's annual survey of large institutional lenders, which it defines as firms with a dedicated commercial/multifamily origination platform.[32]

Finally, our analysis of data from the enterprises and two major participants in the multifamily housing financing marketplace—life insurance companies and CMBS lenders—illustrates how these participants' multifamily activities have changed over time. While theenterprises' role in the multifamily housing finance marketplace was about equal to that of the combined total of originations for life insurance companies and CMBS lenders before the financial crisis (2005 through 2006), Fannie Mae and Freddie Mac dominated the marketplace during the height of the crisis (2008 through 2009) as life insurance companies and CMBS lenders significantly reduced their presence in the market.

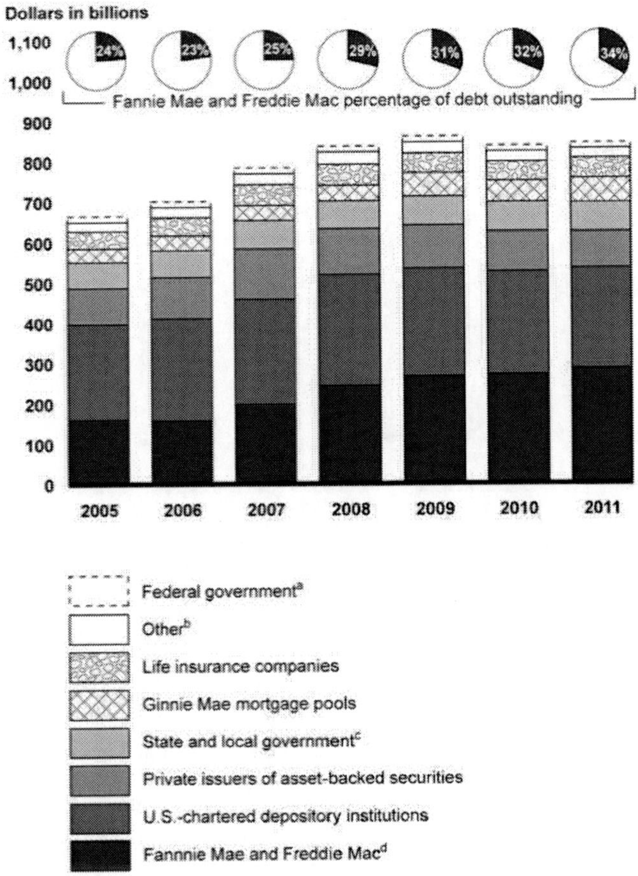

Source: GAO analysis of Federal Reserve data.

[a] Includes multifamily mortgages held by the Farmers Home Administration (currently the Department of Agriculture's Rural Economic and Community Development Service), FHA, the Department of Veterans Affairs, and the Federal Deposit Insurance Corporation.

[b] Other holders include foreign banking offices in the United States, private pension funds, and real estate investment trusts.

[c] Includes retirement funds.

[d] Includes enterprise-backed mortgage pools.

Figure 17. Multifamily Mortgage Debt Outstanding, 2005-2011.

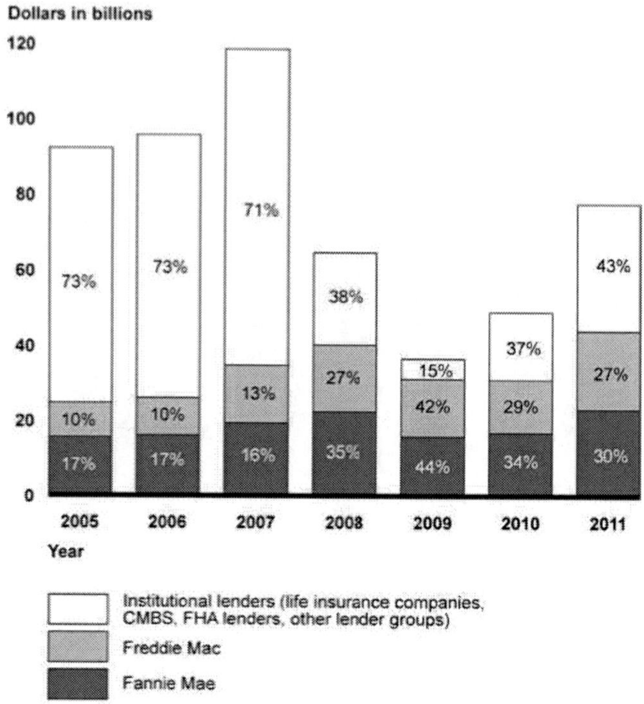

Source: GAO analysis of MBA data.

Note: According to MBA, institutional lenders do not include small banks and thrifts. Percentages may not add to 100 because of rounding.

Figure 18. Financing of Multifamily Loans Originated, 2005-2011.

Data from the enterprises, ACLI, and Trepp show that by 2008, the enterprises' combined purchases were almost $60 billion compared with almost $4 billion for life insurance companies and CMBS lenders combined (see table 2).[33] The data from ACLI and Trepp also showed that life insurance companies and CMBS lenders started reentering the market in 2010.

Few Studies Examined Enterprises' Role in Multifamily Market but Most Noted Positive Effects

Based on our reviews of existing literature and interviews with stakeholders, the enterprises have provided access to multifamily financing although some view their role in the small-loan market segment as limited. Our review of the available literature on the role the enterprises have played in the secondary market for multifamily housing revealed few studies on this issue, partly due to the long-standing emphasis on Fannie Mae and Freddie Mac's single-family portfolios.

Table 2. Principal Balance of Multifamily Loans Purchased by the Enterprises and Multifamily Loans Originated by Life Insurance Companies and CMBS Lenders, 2005-2011

Acquisition or origination year	Fannie Mae (dollars in millions)[a]	Freddie Mac (dollars in millions)a	Life insurance companies (dollars in millions)[b]	CMBS lenders (dollars in millions)[b]
2005	$22,844	$10,768	$7,636	$21,837
2006	22,233	12,669	11,167	27,399
2007	46,297	22,644	9,709	32,750
2008	34,691	24,165	2,872	1,087
2009	19,537	17,063	564	0
2010	16,832	14,508	4,651	380
2011	24,177	19,993	11,136	1,319

Sources: GAO analysis of Fannie Mae and Freddie Mac data; ACLI; and Trepp.

[a]The amounts for Fannie Mae and Freddie Mac are the unpaid principal balance on loans acquired each year and are not adjusted for inflation.

[b]The amounts for life insurance companies and CMBS lenders are the original principal balance on loans originated each year and are not adjusted for inflation.

Additionally, the studies we found generally lacked both empirical research and a balanced analysis of the benefits and costs of the enterprises. This was driven, in part, by the lack of publicly available data on the enterprises' multifamily activities and on the multifamily housing finance marketplace as a whole.

However, the available literature we reviewed included statements that the enterprises have provided liquidity, stability, and affordability.[34] For example, five of the seven studies we reviewed stated that the enterprises have helped ensure a robust financing system for multifamily housing by providing vital liquidity and counter-cyclical stability, but did not include empirical evidence supporting these statements.[35] According to these studies, Fannie Mae and Freddie Mac have provided capital to the secondary mortgage market for multifamily financing during all economic climates, including times of credit market stress. One study cited certain instances in which the enterprises had provided liquidity (in the wake of the currency crisis in 1998, after the 2001 recession, and in 2007 through 2008 when purely private sources withdrew or charged untenable interest rates).[36]

Most mortgage finance and housing policy groups with whom we spoke generally agreed that the enterprises had provided liquidity and counter-cyclical stability. They agreed that the enterprises were a major source of funding for multifamily projects during the recent financial crisis. According to one group, the flight of traditional providers of private capital (such as banks and life insurance companies) would have been more devastating to renters had it not been for the enterprises' presence.

The five studies we cited previously also stated that the enterprises generally promoted access to affordable rental housing. As discussed in more detail later in this report, the enterprises must meet affordable housing goals for targeted groups such as low- and moderate-income households. One study stated, "the government's involvement in ensuring that capital is available during times of credit contraction is a critical factor in mitigating fluctuations in the supply of market-rate and affordably priced rental housing."[37] All five studies discussed the role the enterprises have played in the LIHTC program. For example, one housing policy group wrote that the enterprises have acted both as equity investors and purchasers of mortgages for affordable housing developments financed by the LIHTC program.[38] It noted that through their loan purchases, the enterprises facilitated 15-year, fixed-rate mortgages that were essential for these tax credits to be attractive to LIHTC investors. However, the studies also noted that with no income tax liability to shelter, Fannie Mae and Freddie Mac have withdrawn from the LIHTC investment market. According to FHFA, it instructed the enterprises to withdraw from the LIHTC market. Although it is no longer an active equity investor, Freddie Mac officials noted that the enterprise continues to purchase and guarantee mortgages that support LIHTC programs.

While representatives of most of the groups we interviewed stated that Fannie Mae and Freddie Mac generally had played a role in providing access to affordable rental housing, they emphasized that the enterprises could do more. For example, one association told us that the affordable housing goal levels are generally set too low. In its comment letter on FHFA's proposed rule on the 2010 and 2011 affordable housing goals, it wrote that Fannie Mae and Freddie Mac actually had been doing even less to finance what it called legitimate, affordable rental housing since conservatorship. The association provided as an example the experience of one of its members, a lending consortium whose funds came from a pool of 45 investors. One of the enterprises had been an investor since 1993, but recently had been the only major investor to not renew its commitment. According to this enterprise, FHFA has directed it to cease making certain types of investments and loans.

In addition, our literature review and interviews indicated that the enterprises have played a limited role in financing small multifamily properties, which tend to have lower rents than larger properties. According to the 2010 American Community Survey, almost one-third of renters live in structures with 5 to 49 units (see fig. 19).

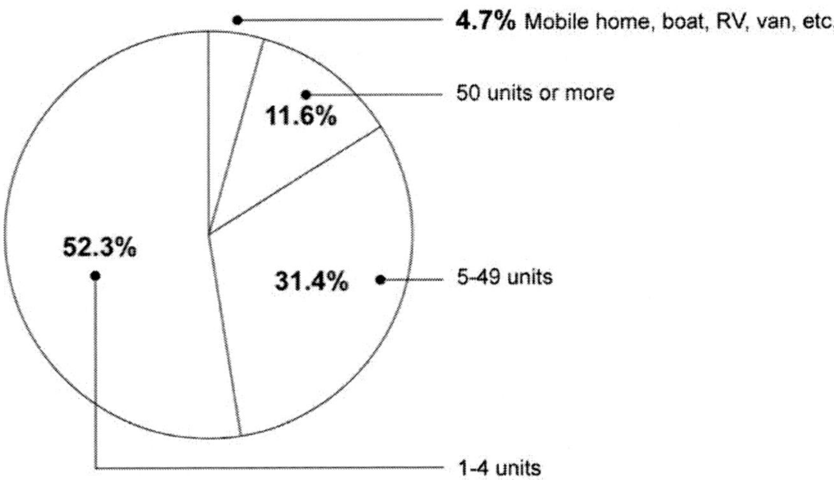

Source: GAO analysis of American Community Survey data.

Note: The American Community Survey data used do not include unoccupied rental units.

Figure 19. Distribution of Rental Units by Building Size (Number of Units), 2010.

Representatives from trade associations, housing policy groups, industry researchers, and a consumer advocacy group generally agreed on the limited role that Fannie Mae and Freddie Mac played in the small-loan market segment. For example, two trade associations stated that enterprise financing generally has not flowed outside major metropolitan areas, where there is a need for small-loan financing. In its comment letter on FHFA's proposed rule on the 2010 and 2011 affordable housing goals, one of these trade associations stated that smaller-sized properties that are affordable to low- and moderate-income persons are the most underserved segment of the multifamily market, in large part because of low levels of enterprise activity in this market segment.

As previously noted, small loans (those for properties with 5 to 50 units) make up a small percentage of the loans that the enterprises have purchased.[39] According to Fannie Mae's 2011 activity report, 22,382 of the 390,526 multifamily units that Fannie Mae financed (5.7 percent) were through small loans. Of these multifamily units, 76 percent were low-income or very low-income rental units.[40] According to Freddie Mac's 2011 activity report, the enterprise's units financed through small loans comprised 0.7 percent of the multifamily units it financed (2,173 of 290,116 units). About 35 percent of these units were low-income or very low-income rental units. Although well below the enterprises' participation in the larger property market, officials at FHFA, Fannie Mae, and Freddie Mac contend that the enterprises' small-loan activity levels are noteworthy because this segment of the market has been dominated by banks and thrifts—institutions that have greater familiarity with local needs. (For information on how the size of the loans that the enterprises purchased compares with the size of loans financed by other major participants in the multifamily housing financing marketplace, see app. IV.)

While most studies we reviewed and individuals we interviewed stated that the enterprises played an important role in multifamily housing finance, two studies stated that private capital should play a larger role. The first study concluded that without the enterprises over the past 20 years, "a fully functioning, private debt financing market for multifamily housing would have existed, in the same way that fully private debt financing markets exist for office, retail, and industrial properties."[41] According to the study, the multifamily market is dependent on the enterprises because of a lack of competition among other lenders, derived from the enterprises' unfair pricing advantages. Similarly, the second study stated that before the enterprises' involvement, life insurance companies, pension funds, and banks supported a robust conventional multifamily lending market.[42] According to the study, once the enterprises entered the multifamily market, the private sector had an increasingly difficult time competing with the enterprises because their charter provided them with certain advantages, such as pricing. The authors of the first study and other stakeholders we interviewed stated that the benefits conferred on Fannie Mae and Freddie Mac by their status as government-sponsored entities created a competitive advantage over other market participants, temporarily crowding them out of the market.

In February 2012, FHFA released a strategic plan for the enterprises' single- and multifamily operations during the next phase of conservatorship. In the plan, FHFA asked Fannie Mae and Freddie Mac to conduct a market analysis of the viability of their multifamily operations without government guarantees. FHFA also released a draft strategic plan for 2013 through 2017, which includes the strategic plan for conservatorship. This plan noted that the enterprises would be working to further standardize the process for securitizing mortgages.[43] According to Fannie Mae and Freddie Mac officials, both enterprises have begun their market analyses and expect to meet FHFA's deadline of December 31, 2012.

Currently, the enterprises compose the largest share of the multifamily market as they and other federal entities compose most of the single-family market. While markets are expected to eventually recover from the financial crisis, the future role of the enterprises is unknown due to a number of factors. However, our analysis of multifamily funding activity over time provides insight into the role the enterprises have played in the marketplace during periods in which the markets were relatively stable. For example, prior to the financial crisis, our analysis revealed that the enterprises generally financed about 30 percent of multifamily mortgages.

Enterprises' Multifamily Activities Are Important to Meeting Affordable Housing Goal Requirements

Beginning in 2010, FHFA implemented the Housing and Economic Recovery Act of 2008 (HERA) by making significant changes to the housing goal framework, including establishing separate goals for the purchases of single- and multifamily mortgages.

HUD and FHFA Roles and Responsibilities

The Safety and Soundness Act required the enterprises to meet annual numeric goals for the purchase of mortgages serving targeted groups.[44] Specifically, the act established three broad affordable housing goals for Fannie Mae and Freddie Mac: (1) a broad low- and moderate-income goal for families earning less than the area median income (AMI); (2) a geographically targeted goal for housing located in underserved areas, such as central cities and rural areas; and (3) a special affordable housing goal, which targets housing that is affordable to very low-income families and low-income families living in low-income areas. In HUD's first rulemaking on the affordable housing goals, it defined underserved areas as census tracts with median income at or below 90 percent of AMI in metropolitan areas and 95 percent of AMI in nonmetropolitan areas, or high-minority areas (metropolitan census tracts in which at least 30 percent of households are minority and the tract median income does not exceed 120 percent of AMI).[45] The special affordable goal targeted borrowers or renters earning no more than 60 percent of AMI or earning no more than 80 percent of AMI and residing in census tracts with median income at or below 80 percent of AMI.

The Safety and Soundness Act required HUD to consider several factors in establishing these housing goals, including: (1) national housing needs; (2) economic, housing, and demographic conditions; (3) past performance on each goal; (4) the size of the corresponding primary mortgage market; (5) the ability of the enterprises to lead the industry, and (6) the need to maintain the sound financial condition of the enterprises. For the period 1993 through 2008, HUD considered past performance and the size of the corresponding primary market as the two primary factors when setting the goals.[46]

The enterprises could purchase both single- and multifamily mortgages to satisfy these goals. Starting in 1996, HUD established a dollar-based special affordable multifamily subgoal related to purchases of multifamily mortgages for properties affordable to very low-income tenants (no more than 60 percent of AMI) or in low-income neighborhoods and affordable to low-income tenants. See figure 20 for information on changes made to the affordable housing goals since they were first set in 1992.

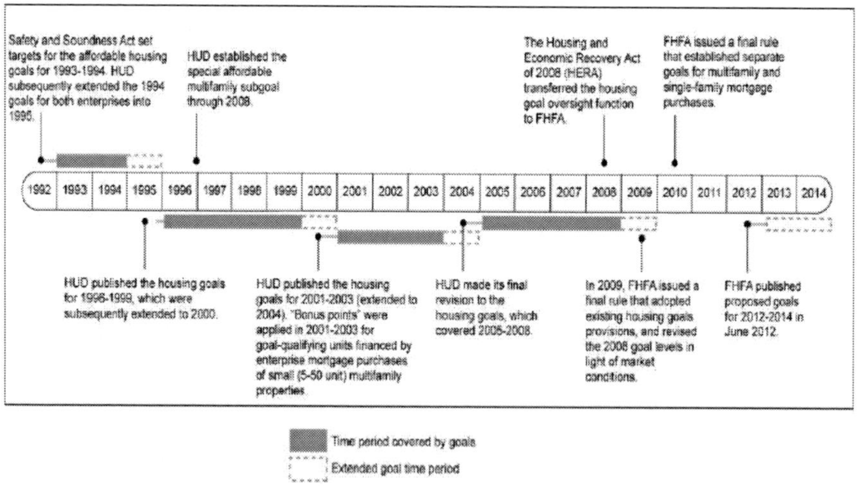

Source: GAO analysis of HUD and FHFA documents.

Figure 20. Enterprises' Affordable Housing Goals Timeline, 1992-2012.

HUD oversaw the enterprises' compliance with the housing goals through 2008. On July 30, 2008, HERA transferred the housing goal oversight function to FHFA.[47] The Safety and Soundness Act, as amended by HERA, requires FHFA to consider the following when setting multifamily goals: national multifamily mortgage credit needs and the ability of the enterprises in making mortgage credit available to provide additional liquidity and stability for the multifamily mortgage market; the performance and effort of the enterprises in making mortgage credit available for multifamily housing in previous years; the size of the multifamily mortgage market for housing affordable to low-income and very low-income families; the ability of the enterprises to lead the market in making multifamily mortgage credit available; the availability of public subsidies; and the need to maintain the sound financial conditions of the enterprises.[48]

In establishing affordable housing goals under HERA, FHFA focused more on the role of the enterprises in the multifamily market given current market conditions and competitors' roles and less on past performance. In August 2009, FHFA issued a final rule that kept many of the existing housing goals provisions, but revised the levels of the existing affordable housing goals downward in light of current market conditions.[49] Beginning in 2010, FHFA, implementing HERA, made significant changes to the goals framework, such as separating the goals for multifamily and single-family mortgage purchases.[50] In its final rule on the affordable housing goals for 2010 and 2011, the agency also redefined the goal targets to reach lower-income groups and required the enterprises to report on their acquisition of mortgages involving low-income units in small (5 to 50 unit) multifamily properties.[51] Further, FHFA prohibited the enterprises from crediting purchases of private-label securities, including CMBS, toward housing goals. On June 11, 2012, FHFA issued a proposed rule on the affordable housing goals for 2012 through 2014.[52] FHFA is proposing to continue the existing structure, with revised single-family and multifamily housing goal benchmark levels for 2012, 2013, and 2014.

The Safety and Soundness Act (as amended by HERA) also requires FHFA's director to annually determine the performance of each enterprise in meeting the housing goals, and determine the feasibility (given current market conditions) of any housing goals and subgoals that an enterprise failed to meet.[53] The enterprises submit quarterly reports to FHFA on goal performance that include loan-level data, as well as an annual report at the end of each year.54 FHFA uses these data to determine official goal performance. If an enterprise fails to attain a goal, the FHFA director may require submission of a housing plan describing the specific action that the enterprise will take to achieve the goal for the next year.[55]

Enterprises' Goal Performance

The enterprises generally have met their affordable housing goals. According to HUD documents, the enterprises generally exceeded their affordable housing goals from 1993 through 2000, with their performance generally increasing during that time period.[56] Official reports on goal performance for 2001 through 2009 show that Fannie Mae and Freddie Mac exceeded their goals from 2001 through 2007, but failed to meet some of the goals in 2008 and 2009 (see table 3). FHFA determined that the two goals both enterprises failed to meet in 2008 (the low- and moderate-income and special affordable goals) were infeasible due to structural changes in the market from 2006 through 2008, which were not anticipated in 2004 when HUD established the goals. Specifically, FHFA took into consideration such factors as tightened underwriting standards in the mortgage industry, the decreased availability of private mortgage insurance in the primary market, the increase in the share of single-family mortgages insured by FHA, and the fall in the issuance of goals-qualifying, private-label securities. Freddie Mac also did not meet the underserved areas goal in 2008.

Table 3. Enterprises' Goal Targets and Performance, 2001-2009

	Low- and moderate-income			Special affordable goal			Underserved areas goal		
Year	Goal (%)	Fannie Mae	Freddie Mac	Goal (%)	Fannie Mae	Freddie Mac	Goal (%)	Fannie Mae	Freddie Mac
2001	50	51.5	53.2	20	21.6	22.6	31	32.6	31.7
2002	50	51.8	50.3	20	21.4	20.5	31	32.8	31
2003	50	52.3	51.2	20	21.2	21.4	31	32.1	32.7
2004	50	53.4	51.6	20	23.6	22.7	31	33.5	32.3
2005	52	55.1	54	22	26.3	24.3	37	41.4	42.3
2006	53	56.9	55.9	23	27.8	26.4	38	43.6	42.7
2007	55	55.5	56.1	25	26.8	25.8	38	43.4	43.1
2008[a]	56	*53.7*	*51.5*	27	*26.4*	*23.1*	39	39.4	*37.7*
2009[b]	43	47.6	44.7	18	20.7	*17.7*	32	*28.8*	*26.8*

Source: FHFA.

[a] For 2008, FHFA declared the low- and moderate-income and special affordable goals infeasible.

[b] For 2009, FHFA determined that the underserved areas goal was not feasible.

Although FHFA determined that the market conditions that made the other two goals infeasible made meeting the underserved areas goal more difficult for Freddie Mac, it did not declare this goal to be infeasible for Freddie Mac. But based on Freddie Mac's financial condition in 2008, FHFA did not require Freddie Mac to submit a housing plan.

FHFA also declared that the underserved areas goal that both enterprises failed to meet in 2009 was infeasible. In making this determination, FHFA considered the same factors it took into account the previous year. Freddie Mac also did not meet the special affordable goal in 2009. FHFA determined that this goal was feasible for Freddie Mac, but in light of the near achievement of the goal, did not require a housing plan.

As noted previously, both enterprises also had to meet a special affordable multifamily subgoal in 2001 through 2009. Fannie Mae and Freddie Mac exceeded this subgoal in each year except for 2009 (see table 4). FHFA declared each enterprise's subgoal for that year to be infeasible after considering the collapse of the CMBS market and the financial condition of the enterprises.[57]

Table 4. Enterprises' Target and Performance for Special Affordable Multifamily Subgoal, 2001-2009

Year	Fannie Mae		Freddie Mac	
	Goal (dollars in billions)	Performance (dollars in billions)	Goal (dollars in billions)	Performance (dollars in billions)
2001	$2.85	$7.36	$2.11	$4.65
2002	2.85	7.57	2.11	5.22
2003	2.85	12.23	2.11	8.79
2004	2.85	7.32	2.11	7.77
2005	5.49	10.39	3.92	12.35
2006	5.49	13.31	3.92	13.58
2007	5.49	19.84	3.92	15.12
2008	5.49	13.31	3.92	7.49
2009	6.56	6.42	4.60	3.69

Source: FHFA.

When the single-family and multifamily goals were combined, the enterprises' multifamily activities were "goal rich," meaning that purchasing multifamily mortgages had a disproportionate importance for the housing goals because most multifamily rental units are occupied by households with low and moderate incomes. For example, in 2008 the enterprises' multifamily business, which represented 4.5 percent of the enterprises' total unpaid principal balance financed, accounted for 32 percent of the units that met the low- and moderate-income goal, 27 percent of the units that met the underserved areas goal, and 39 percent of the units that met the special affordable goal (see table 5).[58]

Table 5. Multifamily Contributions to Enterprises' Affordable Housing Goals, 2001- 2009

Year	Percentage of enterprises' total business that wasmultifamily business	Percentage of units that qualified for each goal that were financed by multifamily mortgages		
		Low- and moderate income goal	Underserved areas goal	Special affordable goal
2001	2.0%	23%	19%	32%
2002	1.5	18	15	24
2003	1.7	22	22	29
2004	3.0	21	17	29
2005	3.6	22	18	31
2006	4.8	27	22	38
2007	7.2	33	27	41
2008	4.5	32	27	39
2009	2.8	18	17	22

Source: GAO analysis of FHFA data.

Table 6. Enterprises' Multifamily Goal Targets and Performance, 2010-2011

	Low-income multifamily goal (units)				Very low-income multifamily goal (units)			
	Fannie Mae		Freddie Mac		Fannie Mae		Freddie Mac	
Year	Goal	Performance	Goal	Performance	Goal	Performance	Goal	Performance
2010	177,750	214,997	161,250	161,500	42,750	53,908	21,000	29,656
2011	177,750	301,224	161,250	229,001	42,750	84,244	21,000	35,471

Sources: FHFA, Fannie Mae, and Freddie Mac.

Note: The numbers for 2011 are preliminary figures reported by Fannie Mae and Freddie Mac in their March 2012 activity reports. FHFA has yet to publish the official numbers for 2011.

For 2010, FHFA established two specific multifamily goals. The low-income multifamily goal was targeted at rental units in multifamily properties affordable to families with incomes no greater than 80 percent of AMI, and the very low-income multifamily subgoal was for units affordable to families with incomes no greater than 50 percent of AMI. Both enterprises' performance levels exceeded the two multifamily goal targets in 2010 and 2011 (see table 6).

ENTERPRISES' PURCHASED MULTIFAMILY LOANS HAVE PERFORMED RELATIVELY WELL, BUT REGULATORS IDENTIFIED ISSUES WITH CREDIT RISK MANAGEMENT

The enterprises have purchased multifamily loans that have underwriting standards and loan performance that compared favorably with those of other market participants. For example, from 2005 through 2010, the enterprises experienced lower default rates than the other major mortgage capital sources, with the exception of life insurance companies. To help offset some of their credit risks and increase the supply of affordable multifamily housing, the enterprises have risk-sharing programs with FHA and RHS.[59] However, these programs involve relatively few loans. OFHEO and FHFA, through their examination and oversight of the enterprises, identified a number of credit risk deficiencies since 2006. For example, they found deficiencies in Fannie Mae's delegated underwriting and servicing program, its risk-management reorganization, and information systems; and Freddie Mac's management of its lower-performing assets. Both enterprises are taking steps to address these deficiencies.

Enterprises' Multifamily Underwriting Standards and Serious Delinquency Rates Compared Favorably with Those of Other Sources of Multifamily Credit

Based on underwriting standards and loan performance, the loans the enterprises purchased generally performed as well as and oftentimes better than other major sources of financing for multifamily housing. The major sources include life insurance companies, CMBS lenders, banks and thrifts, and FHA and RHS lenders.[60] We compared the enterprises' credit standards to those of CMBS lenders and life insurance companies, two major participants in the multifamily housing financing marketplace.[61] From 2005 through 2011, the enterprises' underwriting standards—as measured by median debt-service coverage and LTV ratios—were generally stricter than CMBS lenders.[62] Higher debt-service coverage ratios and lower LTV ratios indicate lower risk. For example, from 2005 through 2011, the enterprises' median debt-service coverage ratios were always higher than those of CMBS lenders, with the exception of Fannie Mae in 2007 (see table 7). Also, over this period, Fannie Mae's LTV ratios were lower than those of CMBS lenders for every year except 2010, while Freddie Mac's LTV ratios were lower than those of CMBS lenders in 3 years. When compared with life insurance company ratios, Fannie Mae's median debt-service coverage ratios were lower for every year from 2005 through 2011, except for 2009. In contrast, Freddie Mac had higher median debt-service coverage ratios than life insurance companies for 3 of the 7 years. In addition, Fannie Mae had lower LTV ratios than life insurance companies for all years except 2008 and 2011, while Freddie Mac had higher LTV ratios than life insurance companies in all years from 2005 through 2011.

Table 7. Median Debt-Service Coverage and LTV Ratios for Multifamily Loans Financed by the Enterprises, CMBS Lenders, and Life Insurance Companies, 2005-2011

Acquisition or origination year	Median debt-service coverage ratio				Median LTV ratio			
	Fannie Mae	Freddie Mac	CMBS lenders	Life insurance companies	Fannie Mae	Freddie Mac	CMBS lenders	Life insurance companies
2005	1.40	1.55	1.33	1.55	62.00	75.00	74.80	69.53
2006	1.35	1.48	1.25	1.37	60.00	70.91	73.90	68.49
2007	1.22	1.39	1.25	1.36	55.00	72.00	74.87	67.48
2008	1.35	1.45	1.22	1.57	64.00	71.84	75.00	59.59
2009	1.36	1.57	N/A	1.34	65.00	70.00	N/A	66.75
2010	1.44	1.55	1.41	1.56	65.00	71.69	63.94	66.32
2011	1.42	1.63	1.40	1.66	65.00	70.23	69.60	63.65

Sources: GAO analysis of Fannie Mae and Freddie Mac data; ACLI; and Trepp.

Note: For Fannie Mae and Freddie Mac, the year represents the year the loan was acquired. For CMBS lenders and life insurance companies, the year is the year the loan was originated. CMBS lenders did not originate any multifamily loans in 2009. According to ACLI, the vast majority of loans that life insurance companies originate are fixed-interest amortizing loans. It noted that other types of multifamily loans may have better debt-service coverage and LTV ratios even though they may be riskier debt.

We also obtained data on credit standards from six HFAs and three loan consortiums.

The median debt-service coverage ratios for five of the HFAs were generally lower than those of the enterprises.[63] For example, from 2005 through 2011, the median debt-service coverage ratios for the five HFAs ranged from 0.92 to 1.72. Likewise, the median debt-service coverage ratios for the three loan consortiums were lower than the ratios for both of the enterprises over this same period. When we compared the median LTV ratios of the six HFAs and the enterprises, we found that three HFAs generally had lower LTV ratios than both of the enterprises for all years from 2005 through 2011, two had LTV ratios that varied compared with those of the enterprises, and one HFA had LTV ratios that were higher than the enterprises. Data from two of the loan consortiums showed that one had median LTV ratios that were lower than those of both enterprises for all years from 2005 through 2011.[64] The second had ratios that were higher than Fannie Mae, but lower than Freddie Mac in 3 of the 7 years. For more information on the credit standards of these HFAs and loan consortiums, see appendix V.

When comparing the performance of multifamily loans financed by Fannie Mae and Freddie Mac with those financed by other major sources of multifamily credit, we were not always able to make direct comparisons because market participants track delinquencies in different ways. We generally found that from 2005 through 2010, the enterprises experienced lower default rates than the other major mortgage capital sources, with the exception of life insurance companies in some cases. For example, as of December 31, 2011, Fannie Mae's serious delinquency rates (loans 60 days or more delinquent) for only those loans acquired or guaranteed in 2005 through 2007 ranged from 0.66 to 0.89 percent (see table 8).

As of the same date, Freddie Mac's serious delinquency rates for loans acquired or guaranteed during this period ranged from 0.20 to 0.74 percent. These rates are considerably lower than the serious delinquency rates for loans originated by CMBS lenders in 2005 through 2007, which peaked at about 24 percent for loans originated in 2007.[65]

Starting in 2008, the serious delinquency rates for loans originated each year by CMBS lenders dropped considerably. FHA's serious delinquency rates for loans originated in 2005 through 2010 were much higher than either of the enterprises for three of the six years. FHA's highest delinquency rate was for 2009, with loans originated that year having a serious delinquency rate of more than 5 percent, compared to a negligible delinquency rate for the enterprises' loans acquired that year.

Table 8. Percentage of Enterprise, CMBS, and FHA Multifamily Loans Financed in 2005-2010 That Were Seriously Delinquent as of December 31, 2011

Acquisition or origination year	Fannie Mae	Freddie Mac	CMBS lenders	FHA lenders
2005	0.73%	0.20%	5.60%	1.19%
2006	0.66	0.25	13.63	0.66
2007	0.89	0.74	23.94	0.54
2008	1.12	0.09	4.68	2.74
2009	0.05	0.00	N/A	5.15
2010	0.04	0.00	0.00	0.02

Sources: Fannie Mae, Freddie Mac, Trepp, and FHA.

Note: Fannie Mae, Freddie Mac, and CMBS and FHA lenders consider loans to be seriously delinquent when they are 60 days or more delinquent. For Fannie Mae and Freddie Mac, the year represents the year the loan was acquired. For CMBS and FHA lenders, the year is the year the loan was originated. CMBS lenders did not originate any multifamily loans in 2009.

Table 9. Percentage of Outstanding Unpaid Principal Balances of Multifamily Loans That Were Seriously Delinquent for the Enterprises and FDIC Banks, Year End 2005- 2011

	60 days or more delinquent		90 days or more delinquent[a]
Year end	Fannie Mae	Freddie Mac	FDIC-insured institutions
2005	0.32%	0.00%	0.25%
2006	0.08	0.06	0.53
2007	0.08	0.02	0.76
2008	0.29	0.03	1.77
2009	0.62	0.20	4.43
2010	0.70	0.26	3.78
2011	0.58	0.22	2.53

Sources: GAO analysis of Fannie Mae and Freddie Mac data, and FDIC data.

Note: All of the percentages in the table are based on unpaid principal balance.

[a]Represents the percentage of loans that are past due 90 days or more or that are in nonaccrual status.

The enterprises also performed better than commercial banks and thrifts insured by the Federal Deposit Insurance Corporation (FDIC). FDIC's Quarterly Banking Profile provides information on the multifamily loan performance of insured commercial banks and thrifts based on their total outstanding portfolios at the end of each quarter. Specifically, the profile provides data on loans that are 90 days or more delinquent.[66] As shown in table 9, with the exception of 2005 for Fannie Mae, for the period 2005 through 2011 the percentage of the enterprises' multifamily loans that were delinquent for 60 days or more was always lower than the percentage of bank and thrift loans that were delinquent for 90 days or more. This was the case even though the 60-day delinquency rate is a stricter measure of delinquency than the 90-day rate.

The life insurance companies generally performed better than Fannie Mae, while Freddie Mac's performance was generally comparable to that of life insurance companies.

As shown in table 10, for life insurance companies, the percentage of unpaid principal balance on multifamily loans that was 60 days or more delinquent ranged from 0 to 0.21 percent from 2005 through 2011. Fannie Mae had higher multifamily serious delinquency rates for all the years in the period, while Freddie Mac had rates closer to those of life insurance companies until 2010 and 2011.[67]

Table 10. Percentage of Outstanding Unpaid Principal Balances of Multifamily Loans That Were Seriously Delinquent for the Enterprises and Life Insurance Companies, Year End 2005-2011

	60 days or more delinquent		
Year end	Fannie Mae	Freddie Mac	Life insurance companies
2005	0.32%	0.00%	0.02%
2006	0.08	0.06	0.02
2007	0.08	0.02	0.00
2008	0.29	0.03	0.02
2009	0.62	0.20	0.21
2010	0.70	0.26	0.01
2011	0.58	0.22	0.13

Sources: GAO analysis of Fannie Mae and Freddie Mac data, and ACLI.

Note: All of the percentages in the table are based on unpaid principal balance.

Smaller participants in the multifamily marketplace generally experienced fewer delinquencies. From 2005 through 2011, only 1 of 401 loans guaranteed or financed by RHS was delinquent for 60 days or more. Further, only one of the six HFAs and one of the three loan consortiums reported delinquencies (60 days or more delinquent).

Both reported delinquencies in 2005 and 2006.

Enterprises' Participation in Multifamily Risk-Sharing Programs Has Been Limited

Fannie Mae and Freddie Mac have entered into risk-sharing agreements with FHA and RHS to increase the supply of affordable multifamily housing and help offset some of their credit risk, but these programs have involved relatively few loans. The enterprises participate in two risk-sharing programs with FHA. The first of these programs, known as the "standard" FHA risk-sharing program, started in 1994. Under the program, the enterprises acquire loans for eligible affordable multifamily housing projects (either new construction or rehabilitation).[68] The loans generally are not to exceed $50 million and the term of the mortgage is for 15 years or more. In the event of a loss on a loan, the enterprises assume the primary risk of loss and FHA reimburses them for 50 percent of the loss. In exchange for reimbursing the enterprises, FHA charges them an annual risk-sharing premium of 25 basis points (.25 percent) of the average unpaid principal balance. The second of these programs, the Green Refinance Plus program, was established in 2011 to preserve and improve existing affordable housing by providing financing to renovate or retrofit properties.[69] No less than 5 percent of the principal balance must be used for renovation or energy or water retrofitting, and the term of the loans must be for no less than 10 years. Under the program, HUD assumes the first loss in an amount equal to 4.35 percent of the unpaid principal balance on a defaulted loan plus 50 percent of the balance of the loss on an equal basis with the enterprises. FHA charges the enterprises an annual risk-sharing premium of 40 basis points (.40 percent) of the average unpaid principal balance for loans with terms of 15 years or more.[70]

Since the inception of the risk-sharing programs with FHA, the enterprises have participated in a small number of risk-sharing loans relative to their overall multifamily housing business. As shown in table 11, from 1995 through 2011, Fannie Mae collaborated with FHA on 157 loans with unpaid principal balances of about $750 million.

Over this period, Fannie Mae purchased or guaranteed more than 95,000 loans with unpaid principal balances of $373 billion. According to Fannie Mae, the decline in the use of this program in recent years is due to the drop off in new LIHTC financings after Fannie Mae and Freddie Mac ceased investing in projects eligible for LIHTCs. As of July 2012, Fannie Mae lenders had closed two Green mortgage loans with unpaid principal balances of $23 million.[71] From 2005 through 2011, Freddie Mac collaborated with FHA on 59 loans or credit-enhanced bonds with unpaid principal balances of $298 million.

Over this period, Freddie Mac purchased or guaranteed more than 9,000 loans with unpaid principal balances of $129 billion.

Table 11. Enterprises' Multifamily Risk-Sharing Loans with FHA, 1995-2011

Acquisition year	Unpaid principal balance (dollars in millions)	Number of loans	Unpaid principal balance (dollars in millions)	Number of loans
1995	$8	1	not available	not available
1996	8	2	not available	not available
1997	12	4	not available	not available
1998	28	7	not available	not available
1999	33	7	not available	not available
2000	41	8	not available	not available
2001	43	7	not available	not available
2002	111	24	not available	not available
2003	82	20	not available	not available
2004	80	24	not available	not available
2005	63	21	$42	8
2006	45	12	77	15
2007	12	3	3	1
2008	16	5	2	1
2009	5	2	67	15
2010	8	2	24	7
2011	157	8	83	12
Total	$752	157	$298	59

Sources: GAO analysis of Fannie Mae data, and Freddie Mac.

Note: Fannie Mae's data only represent loans that are currently on the books. Freddie Mac's data represent loans and credit-enhanced bonds with HUD/FHA risk sharing.

The enterprises also have entered into risk-sharing agreements with RHS, but to a lesser extent than with FHA. Under the enterprises' risk-sharing agreement with the RHS loan guarantee program (known as 538 loans), RHS will guarantee up to 90 percent of the loan. According to RHS, the only risk to the enterprises would be due to nonperformance by the lender. From 2004 through 2011, Fannie Mae purchased and securitized four loans under the RHS program, with unpaid principal balances of more than $7 million. From 2001 through 2011, Freddie Mac purchased and securitized three loans or bonds with RHS, with unpaid principal balances of $6 million as of the end of 2011.

As noted previously, the enterprises also have supported state and local HFAs by providing credit enhancements to tax-exempt bonds used to finance affordable multifamily housing. We interviewed selected state and local HFAs and in general, they viewed the enterprises as important players in providing liquidity for affordable multifamily properties. For example, officials from a large local HFA told us that the enterprises have played a critical role in providing liquidity and long-term credit enhancement to affordable and market-rate developments. According to an official from a small state HFA, before 2008 Fannie Mae was an active and highly valued buyer of their small tax-exempt private activity bonds. The official added that the ability to sell bonds under $5 million on a direct placement basis to Fannie Mae was extremely helpful and has been missed. Allowing Fannie Mae and Freddie Mac to reenter the bond market with private placements would be a significant benefit, and would allow the HFA to provide reliable and dependable financing options to their multifamily affordable housing projects, according to this HFA official. The enterprises have also participated in two temporary Treasury HFA initiatives: (1) the Temporary Credit and Liquidity Facilities (TCLF) program and (2) the New Issue Bond Program (NIBP). TCLF, which provides replacement credit enhancement and liquidity support to outstanding HFA variable-rate demand bonds, is set to expire in 2015. The multifamily NIBP was established to facilitate the purchase of newly issued HFA bonds, the proceeds of which would be used to finance multifamily projects under each participating HFA's program. In general, Treasury sets the pricing parameters and agrees to take the first loss of principal up to 35 percent. The enterprises participate in the program on a 50-50 loss-sharing basis with each other after the top loss coverage by Treasury.

Regulators Have Identified a Number of Deficiencies in Multifamily Credit Risk Management

From 2006 through 2011, FHFA and its predecessor, OFHEO, identified deficiencies in management of credit risk at the enterprises. FHFA oversees the enterprises' credit risk management through on-site examinations and off-site monitoring. As part of its annual on-site examination of the safety and soundness of the enterprises, FHFA assesses their enterprise risk, which includes credit, market, and operational risk.[72] The written report that FHFA submits to Congress by June 15 of each year describes the financial safety and soundness of each enterprise, including the results and conclusions from annual examinations.[73] FHFA also can conduct targeted examinations, which are in-depth, focused evaluations of a specific risk or risk-management system. Throughout the year, FHFA conducts ongoing supervision of the enterprises that includes on-site and off-site monitoring and analyzing of each enterprise's overall business profile, including trends or emerging risks.

FHFA's Division of Enterprise Regulation prepares quarterly risk assessments that inform an Interim Supervisory Assessment Letter, which provides FHFA's view of the condition of the enterprise midway through the examination cycle.

FHFA documents deficiencies identified in examinations or ongoing supervision in a conclusion letter that communicates findings, conclusions, and the assigned supervisory rating.[74]

FHFA is to follow up on deficiencies to ensure that the enterprise's response is appropriate, timely, and effective.

Fannie Mae's Multifamily Credit Risk Challenges

Since 2006, OFHEO and FHFA have identified a number of deficiencies with Fannie Mae's management of multifamily credit risk, including several weaknesses in oversight of its DUS program.[75] Specifically, in OFHEO's 2006 Annual Report to Congress, the agency reported that Fannie Mae's underwriting standards needed updating because of the volume of waivers granted to DUS lenders.

According to OFHEO, the high waiver rate was indicative of a policy that was too restrictive, lending practices that were too liberal, or a policy that was not current relative to market conditions.

And while Fannie Mae authorized DUS lenders to review and approve waivers, the enterprise had not established a strong and comprehensive quality control process. In 2011, FHFA communicated supervisory concerns related to Fannie Mae's DUS program.

Fannie Mae reported that it was taking several steps to address these deficiencies, including training its credit underwriting staff, conducting due diligence and credit analysis for DUS transactions, and expanding its monitoring of multiple loans with the same entity. FHFA noted that the steps Fannie Mae planned to take appeared reasonable but indicated that the enterprise must show that it had implemented these changes and that they could be sustained.

In addition to deficiencies in the DUS program, OFHEO and FHFA identified deficiencies with Fannie Mae's multifamily quality control function, asset management (that is, how it manages loans it acquires), underwriting practices, and information systems supporting credit risk management:

- OFHEO reported in 2006 that Fannie Mae faced deficiencies with its quality control function because Fannie Mae's oversight focused on reviewing documents rather than analyzing and assessing credit information. OFHEO noted that credit information was incomplete or not readily available. In 2007, OFHEO reported that the multifamily quality-control process was improved and expanded to provide better coverage of multifamily loans.
- In 2008, OFHEO reported that Fannie Mae had begun to address deficiencies in asset management. Further, in 2010 FHFA reported that Fannie Mae was identifying problem assets earlier, developing workout strategies for problem loans, and managing delinquencies and foreclosed properties to improve the amount recovered on sales of property in markets and minimize losses.
- In 2011, FHFA found that Fannie Mae needed to improve its risk-management practices for multifamily loans. To address this issue, Fannie Mae stated that it planned to review its existing risk-management processes and controls.
- In 2011, FHFA reviewed certain loans and advised Fannie Mae to strengthen its underwriting and quality control practices related to appraisals and verification of financial information. Fannie Mae stated that it would review its procedures and consult with FHFA as it proceeded.
- Additionally, in 2011 Fannie Mae agreed to respond to supervisory concerns relating to waiver and exception monitoring and reporting.Fannie Mae stated that it would analyze the loans that had been granted waivers or extensions to determine if there were correlations between waivers and subsequent loan performance.
- OFHEO reported in 2008 that Fannie Mae's credit review function was understaffed and that information system deficiencies or inefficiencies compromised the enterprises' ability to manage risks. FHFA also identified deficiencies with Fannie Mae's information systems in 2009 and 2010. According to FHFA, Fannie Mae has begun a transformation initiative to centralize data sources and improve data integrity.

Freddie Mac's Multifamily Credit Risk Challenges

We reviewed OFHEO's annual reports to Congress from 1997 through 2008. During this 12-year period, OFHEO did not report any credit risk deficiencies in Freddie Mac's multifamily housing activities. However, since 2009 FHFA has identified deficiencies in Freddie Mac's multifamily asset-management function. For example, FHFA reported in its 2009 Annual Report to Congress that a targeted examination of Freddie Mac's asset-management function had found that the function needed to be strengthened. FHFA noted that the multifamily business unit had begun to address some of the issues identified. In its 2010 Annual Report to Congress, FHFA continued to report on deficiencies with Freddie Mac's asset-management function, including that it was poorly managed and lacked the necessary process and controls to identify, evaluate, and control problem assets. Additionally, the 2010 report noted problems with the multifamily division's management of the problem loan watch list.[76] In this report, FHFA noted that while risk management for multifamily asset management was unsatisfactory, management had corrected or was addressing these issues. According to FHFA officials, these deficiencies have since been addressed and closed.

AGENCY COMMENTS AND OUR EVALUATION

We provided a draft of this report to FHFA, and it provided copies to Fannie Mae and Freddie Mac. FHFA, Fannie Mae, and Freddie Mac provided technical comments, which we incorporated into the report where appropriate

Sincerely yours,
William B. Shear
Director,
Financial Markets and Community Investment

APPENDIX I: OBJECTIVES, SCOPE, AND METHODOLOGY

Our objectives were to determine (1) how Fannie Mae and Freddie Mac's (the enterprises) multifamily loan activities, products, and loan performance have changed over time; (2) the enterprises' role in the multifamily housing financing marketplace and the extent to which they have met their affordable housing goals; and (3) how the enterprises' credit standards and delinquency rates compare with those of other mortgage capital sources and how they have managed credit risk associated with their multifamily housing activities.

To describe how the enterprises' multifamily loan activities, products, and performance have changed, we analyzed loan-level data from Fannie Mae and Freddie Mac for 1994 (the earliest year for which data were available) through 2011. Each enterprise provided data on the characteristics (at acquisition) of the multifamily loans they purchased and data on the performance of loans over time. We used the data to determine how many loans each enterprise purchased each year from 1994 through 2011 and the unpaid principal balance of those loans at the time of acquisition.[1] Because certain Fannie Mae multifamily loan products roll over periodically (which creates a new loan number but does not represent a new acquisition), we used a new acquisition indicator provided by Fannie Mae to identify its acquisitions each year.[2] When fluctuations in purchase volume were identified, we interviewed Fannie Mae and Freddie Mac officials to determine the reasons for these fluctuations. We also analyzed data on each enterprise's annual purchases of multifamily loans to determine the unpaid principal balance of (1) loans that the enterprise expected to hold in portfolio; (2) loans that it expected to securitize (that is, packaging them into mortgage pools to support mortgage-backed securities (MBS)); and (3) bond credit enhancements.[3] For Fannie Mae, securitized loans included MBS and discount MBS. Freddie Mac's securitized portfolio included participation certificates, tax-exempt bond securitization, and K-deals.[4] Because we were unable to use the loan-level data provided by the two enterprises to determine how much of the multifamily MBS they issued were held in portfolio or sold to investors, we asked both enterprises to provide additional information on MBS held in portfolio. Both enterprises were able to provide data on purchases of their own MBS in 2010 and 2011.

In addition, we analyzed each enterprise's annual multifamily loan purchases from 1994 through 2011 as follows:

- *Size of properties financed*—We determined the number and unpaid principal balance of loans purchased each year that financed properties with 5 to 50 units and properties with 51 or more units.
- *Loan size*—We determined the number and unpaid principal balance of loans purchased each year that fell into the following four categories: $0 to less than $5 million, $5 million to less than $50

million, $50 million to less than $100 million, and $100 million or greater.

- *Geography*—We determined the unpaid principal balance of loans acquired each year in the 25 largest metropolitan statistical areas.[5] For Fannie Mae, we limited our analysis to single loans associated with a single property.[6] To determine the percentage of the nation's multifamily stock that was located in these 25 metropolitan areas, we analyzed data from the 2010 American Community Survey. In addition to focusing on the 25 largest metropolitan areas, we also determined the unpaid principal balance of loans acquired in each state (excluding loans associated with multiple properties as described above).
- *Period of the loan*—We determined the number and unpaid principal balance of loans purchased each year that fell into the following four categories: 60 months or fewer, greater than 60 months to less than 120 months, 120 months, and more than 120 months.
- Asset class—We determined the percentage of loans purchased during the 18-year period (based on unpaid principal balance) in the following five asset classes: traditional rental, student, senior, manufactured, and cooperative housing.[7]
- Type of interest rate—We determined the percentage of loans purchased each year (based on unpaid principal balance) that were fixed- and adjustable-rate mortgages.
- Structured finance—We determined the percentage of unpaid principal balance acquired each year that was associated with transactions involving multiple loans or multiple properties.[8]
- Fannie Mae's Delegated Underwriting and Servicing (DUS®) Program—We determined the number and unpaid principal balance of loans that were purchased under the DUS program each year.[9]

For all of the analyses of the enterprises' multifamily loan purchases, we adjusted the dollar amounts for inflation. In addition, for each analysis we did not include loans with missing values.[10] We also analyzed data on the performance of multifamily loans each enterprise purchased from 1994 to 2011 as follows:

- *Serious delinquency rates*—We calculated annual serious delinquency rates by dividing the current unpaid principal balance of loans that were 60 or more days delinquent as of the end of the year by the total outstanding unpaid principal balance as of the end of the year.[11] We also determined the amount of each enterprise's outstanding unpaid principal balance that was 60 or more days delinquent at the end of each year.

- *Loan maturity*—We determined the number and unpaid principal balance of loans that were going to mature within the next 10 years.
- *Serious delinquency rates for loans with varying debt-service*
- *coverage and loan-to-value (LTV) ratios*—We determined the serious delinquency rates for loans with debt-service coverage ratios above and below 1.25 and for loans with LTV ratios above and below 80 percent.

For the loan maturity analysis, we adjusted the dollar amounts for inflation. For each analysis, we did not include loans with missing values.[12]

We also analyzed aggregated multifamily data that both Fannie Mae and Freddie Mac provided on the following:

- real estate-owned (REO) properties from 2002 through 2011 for Fannie Mae and from 1995 through 2011 for Freddie Mac;
- net income from 2002 through 2011 for Fannie Mae and from 2005 through 2011 for Freddie Mac;
- net charge-offs (debts an entity is unlikely to collect) from 2002 through 2011;[13]
- guarantee fees collected from 2002 through 2011; and
- administrative costs from 2002 through 2011 for Fannie Mae and from 2005 through 2011 for Freddie Mac.[14]

To assess the reliability of these data, we interviewed Fannie Mae and Freddie Mac representatives about how they collected data and helped ensure data integrity, and reviewed internal reports on data reliability. We also compared selected enterprise data with information in public filings. In addition, we conducted reasonableness checks on the data to identify any missing, erroneous, or outlying figures. We determined that the data were sufficiently reliable for our purposes.

To determine what information is available about the enterprises' role in the multifamily housing financing marketplace, we analyzed data on Fannie Mae and Freddie Mac's share of the multifamily housing market from 2005 through 2011.[15] First, we analyzed Flow of Funds data (Table L.219, published on June 7, 2012) from the Board of Governors of the Federal Reserve System (Federal Reserve) on multifamily mortgage debt outstanding to determine the enterprises' share of debt holdings.[16] Second, we analyzed data on the financing of multifamily loans originated by large institutional lenders that the Mortgage Bankers Association (MBA) published. MBA gathers these multifamily origination data through a survey and publishes the data in its Annual Commercial/Multifamily Mortgage Bankers Origination Summation. In 2011, 99 firms participated in MBA's survey, including life insurance companies, commercial mortgage-backed securities (CMBS) lenders, lenders that sell loans to Fannie Mae and Freddie Mac, FHA lenders, and other lender groups. The survey did not include small banks and savings and loan associations (thrifts) because they tend to operate as a separate market, according to MBA. Although not comprehensive, the survey data from MBA are the data most often cited when discussing the enterprises' share of the multifamily housing financing marketplace. We assessed the reliability of both types of data—mortgage debt outstanding and multifamily origination data—by interviewing Federal Reserve and MBA representatives, respectively, about the methods they used to collect and help ensure the integrity of the information. We determined that the data were sufficiently reliable for our purposes. We also compared data from the enterprises and two major participants in the multifamily housing financing marketplace—life insurance companies and CMBS lenders—to illustrate how these participants' multifamily activities have changed over time. Specifically, we compared data obtained from the American Council of Life Insurers (ACLI) and Trepp on loans originated from 2005 through 2011 with our analysis of data from Fannie Mae and Freddie Mac on loans purchased during those years.[17] We assessed the reliability of the ACLI and Trepp data by sending them a set of standard data reliability questions and obtaining their written responses. We followed up with them when we had questions on the data or their responses to our data reliability questions. Where possible, we also compared the data they provided to us with published data. We determined that the data were sufficiently reliable for our purposes. To identify reports on the enterprises' role in the multifamily housing financing marketplace, we conducted a search of literature published since 1995 but found few studies that focused on the enterprises' multifamily activities. Ultimately, we identified seven studies that provided varying viewpoints on the role that Fannie Mae and Freddie Mac have played in multifamily housing finance. [18] Although we found that these studies lacked empirical research, we determined that they were sufficiently reliable for our purposes (identifying literature and authors' conclusions and the limitations of the studies). To obtain additional views on the enterprises' role in multifamily housing financing, we met with the authors of two of these studies and with researchers who have knowledge about housing finance and the operations of the enterprises. We also discussed the enterprises' role with representatives from the Federal Housing Finance Agency (FHFA); Fannie Mae; Freddie Mac; other participants in the multifamily housing financing marketplace such as ACLI, the Commercial Real Estate Finance Council (CREFC), the Federal Housing Administration (FHA), MBA, the National Association of Affordable Housing Lenders (NAAHL), the National Council of State Housing Agencies (NCSHA), and the Department of Agriculture's Rural Housing Service (RHS); the National Multi Housing Council; and the Consumer Federation of America. To comment on the enterprises' role in financing loans for small properties (5 to 50 units), we analyzed data from the 2010 American Community Survey on the percentage of renters who live in small multifamily structures and data from the enterprises' 2011 Annual Housing Activity Reports on their purchases of loans for such properties. We reviewed information on the American Community Survey data we used and determined that the data were sufficiently reliable for the purposes of our report.

To report on the extent to which the enterprises have met their affordable housing goals, we reviewed the laws and regulations establishing the goals from 1992 to the present. We also reviewed reports on the affordable housing goals, including GAO reports and reports from the Department of Housing and Urban Development (HUD), FHFA, the Office of Federal Housing Enterprise Oversight (OFHEO), and independent researchers.[19] We relied on HUD documents to assess the enterprises' annual goal performance from 1993 through 2000.[20] For 2001 through 2009, we analyzed data in Annual Housing Activity Reports (activity report) provided by FHFA. To assess the contribution of the enterprises' multifamily activities to achievement of the affordable housing goals from 2001 through 2009, we calculated multifamily purchases as a percentage of the total mortgage purchases used to meet each goal using data from the activity reports. We assessed the reliability of the data used to document goal performance by interviewing FHFA officials and representatives at Fannie Mae and Freddie Mac about the methods they use to collect and help ensure the integrity of the information. We also reviewed internal reports that the enterprises completed related to data reliability. We determined that the data were sufficiently reliable for our purposes.

To compare the enterprises' credit standards and delinquency rates with those of major mortgage capital sources, we analyzed loan-level data on the enterprises' median debt-service coverage and LTV ratios and delinquency rates. We compared these ratios and delinquency rates with those of selected market players:

- For life insurance companies, ACLI provided us with data from 2005 through 2011 on median debt-service coverage ratios, median LTV ratios, the percentage of the outstanding unpaid principal balance that was 60 days or more delinquent as of the end of each year, median loan size, and median number of units per property.
- For CMBS lenders, we obtained data from Trepp for 2005 through 2011 on median debt-service coverage ratios, median LTV ratios, median loan size, median number of units per property, and the percentage of loans 60 days or more delinquent—based on unpaid principal balance—for only those loans originated from 2005 through 2010.
- We obtained data from FHA on the percentage of loans 60 days or more delinquent—based on unpaid principal balance—for only those loans originated from 2005 through 2010.
- We obtained data from RHS for 2005 through 2011 on the number of loans 60 days or more delinquent, the average loan size, and the average units per property.
- For state and local housing finance agencies (HFA), NCSHA helped us obtain data from four state and two local HFAs.21 Specifically, we obtained data on median debt-service coverage ratios, median LTV ratios, percentage of outstanding unpaid principal balances that were 60 days or more delinquent, median loan size, and median number of units per property.[22]
- For loan consortiums, NAAHL helped us obtain data from three consortiums.[23] Specifically, we obtained data for 2005 through 2011 on median debt-service coverage ratios, median LTV ratios, and the percentage of loans 60 days or more delinquent.[24] Additionally, two of the three loan consortiums provided us with data on median loan size and the median number of units per property.

We assessed the reliability of the data provided by these data sources by sending them a set of standard data reliability questions and obtaining their written responses. We followed up with the specific sources of data when we had questions about the data or their responses to our data reliability questions. Where possible, we also compared the data they provided to us with published data. We determined that the data were sufficiently reliable for our purposes. We also interviewed officials from ACLI, CREFC, FHA, RHS, NCSHA, and NAAHL.

To determine the extent to which the enterprises shared risk with FHA and RHS, we obtained loan-level and aggregated data from the enterprises on the number of loans in risk-sharing programs with FHA and RHS. As discussed earlier, we took a number of steps to assess the reliability of the loan-level and aggregated data and determined that the data were sufficiently reliable for our purposes.

To help us understand how these risk-sharing programs operate, we reviewed documents describing the programs, including memorandums of understanding between the enterprises and FHA and RHS. We reviewed documentation on the enterprises' efforts to support state and local HFAs, including the Department of the Treasury's temporary HFA initiative. We also interviewed officials from Fannie Mae, Freddie Mac, FHA, RHS, NCSHA, and selected state and local HFAs to obtain information on their experiences with these programs.

To describe how the enterprises managed credit risk associated with their multifamily activities, we reviewed FHFA's examination reports and OFHEO and FHFA annual reports to Congress, which summarize credit risk issues identified during annual examinations of the enterprises. We also interviewed FHFA officials to obtain information on current credit risk issues.

To describe how the enterprises have addressed or will address these issues, we reviewed the enterprises' formal responses to FHFA's examination reports and any subsequent FHFA responses. Because FHFA's examination reports and the enterprises' responses are confidential, we limited our discussions of them to a summary.

We also made revisions based on concerns FHFA raised with our original language summarizing supervisory concerns expressed in examination reports. We conducted this performance audit from November 2011 to September 2012 in accordance with generally accepted government auditing standards.

Those standards require that we plan and perform the audit to obtain sufficient, appropriate evidence to provide a reasonable basis for our findings and conclusions based on our audit objectives. We believe that the evidence obtained provides a reasonable basis for our findings and conclusions based on our audit objectives.

Table 13 shows Freddie Mac's multifamily loan purchases in the 25 largest MSAs from 1994 through 2011.

APPENDIX II: FANNIE MAE AND FREDDIE MAC'S MULTIFAMILY LOAN PURCHASES IN THE 25 LARGEST METROPOLITAN AREAS

This appendix provides the data that support the interactive maps in this report (figs. 5 and 6). Specifically, table 12 shows Fannie Mae's multifamily loan purchases in the 25 largest metropolitan statistical areas (MSA) from 1994 through 2011.[1]

Table 12. Fannie Mae's Multifamily Loan Purchases in the 25 Largest Metropolitan Areas, 1994-2011 (Numbers in thousands)

MSA	1994	1995	1996	1997	1998	1999	2000	2001	2002	2003	2004	2005	2006	2007	2008	2009	2010	2011
New York-Northern New Jersey-Long Island, NY-NJ-PA	$744,141	$316,137	$1,045,773	$966,751	$1,379,102	$1,247,888	$779,314	$2,377,162	$3,192,993	$5,733,621	$4,303,917	$3,877,184	$4,023,909	$5,456,795	$3,331,178	$1,642,534	$1,602,823	$2,107,160
Los Angeles-Long Beach-Santa Ana, CA	193,155	1,090,211	443,937	427,237	2,728,972	882,790	591,222	2,190,293	3,227,513	7,474,893	2,253,669	3,812,396	2,947,757	5,006,683	4,693,595	2,246,120	2,503,525	1,688,719
Chicago-Joliet-Naperville, IL-IN-WI	159,606	304,689	261,066	202,107	335,301	280,243	248,369	536,809	258,059	553,946	312,787	410,657	405,133	661,342	908,570	445,993	362,785	611,549
Dallas-Fort Worth-Arlington, TX	260,535	283,680	648,148	554,908	559,759	513,918	519,902	797,390	392,798	276,426	349,067	450,081	444,041	678,853	1,068,544	423,324	534,187	1,098,665
Philadelphia-Camden-Wilmington, PA-NJ-DE-MD	90,359	99,101	237,716	90,612	456,009	95,860	153,163	383,988	337,505	655,283	386,825	677,978	531,173	654,429	738,626	434,437	438,469	367,251
Houston-Sugar Land-Baytown, TX	189,002	157,105	191,885	221,139	211,003	292,489	207,980	678,698	474,419	656,017	310,041	320,471	347,096	635,106	695,509	386,099	188,618	447,744

Table 12. (Continued)

MSA	1994	1995	1996	1997	1998	1999	2000	2001	2002	2003	2004	2005	2006	2007	2008	2009	2010	2011
Washington-Arlington-Alexandria, DC-VA-MD-WV	487,909	111,477	260,086	815,911	434,551	369,827	681,352	1,062,119	688,892	675,196	759,981	854,436	666,393	604,191	978,292	837,503	1,224,012	1,368,551
Miami-Fort Lauderdale-Pompano Beach, FL	161,563	187,811	103,843	88,851	165,871	253,629	258,201	539,022	378,649	473,447	248,655	125,296	254,791	305,189	360,493	291,370	349,543	488,996
Atlanta-Sandy Springs-Marietta, GA	207,721	505,419	277,673	198,247	248,780	374,844	542,991	503,549	297,358	333,497	224,567	318,887	307,769	269,413	495,317	180,582	192,989	331,364
Boston-Cambridge-Quincy, MA-NH	25,067	121,465	284,170	83,351	187,234	202,243	111,179	215,387	257,189	552,591	207,520	227,707	355,990	296,435	493,423	223,776	162,777	323,548
San Francisco-Oakland-Fremont, CA	183,764	383,417	204,306	79,335	758,383	337,698	290,418	1,197,640	1,385,614	3,025,069	929,912	1,010,337	703,834	1,902,171	668,051	542,974	670,690	745,012
Detroit-Warren-Livonia, MI	110,677	78,557	187,459	81,634	118,438	187,072	253,395	334,847	216,139	313,633	180,732	183,639	261,046	205,137	306,178	39,272	18,176	122,245
Riverside-San Bernardino-Ontario, CA	57,507	56,322	77,402	65,831	101,698	144,180	140,042	512,921	479,780	599,849	408,861	507,096	215,590	519,422	453,819	383,742	209,733	429,682
Phoenix-Mesa-Glendale, AZ	210,975	132,133	209,013	187,861	329,813	180,843	243,343	291,264	185,562	237,146	239,265	304,002	262,805	276,380	340,706	236,112	265,024	334,577
Seattle-Tacoma, Bellevue, WA	130,902	47,826	284,131	337,617	477,519	461,248	264,806	710,523	445,676	963,368	473,119	795,925	775,228	1,087,787	690,980	503,675	507,754	755,478
Minneapolis-St. Paul-Bloomington, MN-WI	46,588	78,893	93,671	69,360	144,920	93,722	161,660	293,075	338,210	391,891	207,332	339,476	222,441	344,418	232,052	261,294	151,538	267,636
San Diego-Carlsbad-San Marcos, CA	115,646	284,867	96,833	89,659	545,440	199,398	338,029	619,180	576,425	1,875,615	354,079	698,159	387,975	914,426	780,067	464,152	364,279	547,635
St. Louis, MO-IL	30,	61,	60,	100,	123,	74,	22,	50,	178,	168,	65,	129,	172,	214,	184,	44,	118,	138,

MSA	1994	1995	1996	1997	1998	1999	2000	2001	2002	2003	2004	2005	2006	2007	2008	2009	2010	2011
	975	940	222	904	889	390	742	442	155	635	811	096	531	876	667	648	723	239
Tampa-St. Petersburg-Clearwater, FL	43, 636	67, 424	54, 090	19, 133	54, 360	132, 055	153, 703	175, 091	197, 644	182, 369	223, 621	358, 157	177, 865	281, 639	185, 247	115, 731	106, 910	218, 834
Baltimore-Towson, MD	52, 195	86, 834	292, 355	215, 217	225, 269	85, 167	201, 038	246, 974	385, 717	749, 660	463, 337	323, 491	407, 868	483, 970	206, 235	233, 707	193, 216	352, 232
Denver-Aurora-Broomfield, CO	144, 852	130, 556	108, 356	108, 655	293, 959	200, 359	375, 825	301, 975	378, 944	362, 331	94, 183	195, 868	116, 886	296, 874	326, 176	361, 348	408, 563	504, 864
Pittsburgh, PA	11, 258	7, 749	11, 528	22, 065	56, 284	21, 741	21, 628	30, 573	28, 328	12, 452	19, 103	62, 112	37, 662	43, 533	88, 682	37, 857	102, 438	44, 072
Portland-Vancouver-Hillsboro, OR-WA	130, 061	21, 876	64, 558	88, 133	181, 140	142, 531	92, 721	317, 825	147, 658	577, 599	192, 460	209, 527	74, 645	276, 476	284, 889	187, 602	299, 319	363, 801
Sacramento-Arden-Arcade-Roseville, CA	58, 535	114, 800	62, 391	99, 771	208, 988	207, 552	242, 558	590, 909	624, 506	1,100, 782	189, 908	342, 004	309, 785	446, 056	282, 184	256, 999	234, 986	414, 916
San Antonio-New Braunfels, TX	114, 363	33, 425	69, 728	62, 327	158, 068	53, 103	84, 178	146, 315	124, 249	103, 795	146, 853	213, 202	101, 279	188, 455	184, 899	137, 262	90, 626	334, 612
Total	$3, 960,990	$4,763 715	$5,630, 336	$5,276 615	$10,48 4,750	$7,034 787	$6,979, 756	$15,103, 971	$15,19 7,980	$28,049, 113	$13,54 5,606	$16, 747,181	$14,511, 489	$22, 050,054	$18, 978,378	$10,918, 113	$11,301, 703	$14,407, 381

Source: GAO analysis of Fannie Mae data.

Note: All dollar figures are in 2012 dollars. We included only those purchases where a single loan was associated with a single property. As discussed earlier in this report, Fannie Mae offers financing options that can result in one loan for multiple properties, multiple loans for multiple properties, or multiple loans for one property.

Table 13. Freddie Mac's Multifamily Loan Purchases in the 25 Largest Metropolitan Areas, 1994-2011 (Numbers in thousands)

MSA	1994	1995	1996	1997	1998	1999	2000	2001	2002	2003	2004	2005	2006	2007	2008	2009	2010	2011
New York-Northern New Jersey-Long Island, NY-NJPA	$98, 688	$236, 343	$400, 449	$308, 555	$595, 265	$954, 772	$1,144, 572	$1,236, 949	$916, 149	$1,634, 769	$1,179, 272	$1,148, 238	$1,457, 941	$1,539, 477	$1,940, 288	$2,464, 723	$1,589, 207	$1,440, 366
Los Angeles-Long Beach-Santa Ana, CA	92, 853	9, 192	45, 635	55, 712	336, 592	808, 919	570, 388	1,069, 601	1,738, 336	4,560, 043	1,639, 905	489, 965	1,013, 025	1,452, 313	1,581, 290	2,080, 086	878,087	1,323, 208
Chicago-Joliet-Naperville, ILIN-WI	6, 609	55, 753	113, 224	43, 343	121, 094	424, 976	307, 711	206, 089	523, 214	1,110, 551	379, 521	293, 569	396, 899	617, 956	788, 486	357, 806	504, 584	393, 335
Dallas-Fort Worth-Arlington, TX	63, 800	49, 735	112, 891	54, 673	8, 659	381, 015	141, 791	542, 542	658, 402	380, 499	761, 447	876, 955	696, 385	1,301, 356	1,431, 090	809, 458	566, 460	946, 068
Philadelphia-Camden-Wilmington, PA-NJ-DE-MD	38, 257	83, 317	237, 688	118, 309	164, 235	128, 289	125, 509	120, 192	213, 443	196, 386	462, 110	331, 806	326, 157	370, 700	581, 694	225, 782	368, 133	261, 067
Houston-Sugar Land-Baytown, TX	32, 742	18, 585	37, 707	169, 185	74, 981	219, 197	172, 053	249, 732	482, 589	313, 643	183, 060	306, 875	280, 425	777, 784	918, 692	731, 871	581, 965	878, 911
Washington-	86,	61,	69,	189,	200,	700,	555,	513,	662,	547,	702,	430,	1,306,	1,713,	1,786,	1,464,	1,481,	1,885,

MSA	1994	1995	1996	1997	1998	1999	2000	2001	2002	2003	2004	2005	2006	2007	2008	2009	2010	2011
Arlington-Alexandria, DC-VA-MDWV	414	926	220	667	386	749	173	366	132	724	160	358	965	566	065	062	161	826
Miami-Fort Lauderdale-Pompano Beach, FL	37, 303	75, 615	84, 048	68, 594	273, 059	339, 779	141, 099	208, 012	215, 487	286, 767	109, 039	234, 294	216, 749	408, 907	474, 604	402, 362	381, 621	248, 882
Atlanta-Sandy Springs-Marietta, GA	13, 283	114, 478	65, 812	140, 079	159, 881	377, 732	451, 907	631, 652	461, 872	473, 488	587, 299	730, 248	675, 899	1,140, 981	1,432, 816	679, 148	560, 696	769, 227
Boston-Cambridge-Quincy, MA-NH	20, 051	16, 352	45, 657	4, 055	110, 820	108, 227	104, 446	272, 540	254, 871	116, 971	238, 104	139, 834	139, 101	543, 756	402, 123	455, 982	180, 823	237, 770
San Francisco-Oakland-Fremont, CA	0	9, 713	3, 451	225, 249	40, 157	461, 416	50, 408	420, 231	1,064, 658	1,637, 145	625, 352	357, 881	124, 221	767, 933	776, 039	427, 612	396, 735	309, 341
Detroit-Warren-Livonia, MI	11, 756	21, 515	79, 618	34, 719	53, 895	68, 582	82, 242	73, 900	55, 217	84, 801	46, 662	150, 160	105, 028	62, 979	130, 205	12, 350	14, 850	116, 037
Riverside-San Bernardino-Ontario, CA	0	10, 284	8, 970	18, 099	16, 785	71, 381	117, 135	227, 688	183, 831	216, 068	462, 983	236, 340	140, 611	348, 845	374, 126	173, 119	305, 109	368, 436
Phoenix-Mesa-Glendale, AZ	3, 713	29, 776	37, 681	20, 145	58, 423	198, 004	205, 551	210, 905	255, 305	81, 503	264, 117	270, 732	190, 400	293, 416	478, 233	526, 070	401, 121	515, 286

Table 13. (Continued)

MSA	1994	1995	1996	1997	1998	1999	2000	2001	2002	2003	2004	2005	2006	2007	2008	2009	2010	2011
Seattle-Tacoma, Bellevue, WA	6,895	42,784	23,012	78,277	116,133	129,580	129,410	300,944	168,384	222,966	303,461	351,033	176,285	824,566	696,973	529,817	300,879	687,120
Minneapolis-St. Paul-Bloomington, MN-WI	20,424	40,764	43,306	32,595	165,266	281,567	62,932	135,550	228,673	163,454	268,450	259,826	107,813	253,714	385,799	155,550	134,649	77,345
San Diego-Carlsbad-San Marcos, CA	41,136	33,147	29,559	92,727	144,321	208,700	125,447	514,197	630,942	961,244	587,888	170,079	165,347	475,320	606,983	316,492	311,837	321,595
St. Louis, MOIL	0	0	23,466	2,781	6,036	7,222	19,077	84,467	71,250	63,706	26,963	98,264	126,030	288,571	72,309	104,701	42,068	87,124
Tampa-St. Petersburg-Clearwater, FL	3,517	5,505	30,306	24,768	125,093	132,318	90,305	113,869	107,194	71,493	96,610	216,877	110,984	131,451	228,801	250,012	267,510	407,552
Baltimore-Towson, MD	48,712	10,243	68,499	33,501	141,717	286,844	279,298	186,492	187,662	355,031	458,447	444,548	616,001	708,209	350,448	172,733	132,564	386,512
Denver-Aurora-Broomfield, CO	1,351	88,349	69,331	11,883	151,222	184,073	113,067	353,487	244,802	136,900	90,690	120,637	261,103	461,569	522,927	553,949	346,467	578,150
Pittsburgh, PA	0	14,218	21,176	22,789	65,060	17,374	9,568	32,603	40,276	40,932	34,751	22,881	12,318	30,552	57,104	26,531	126,040	38,624
Portland-																		
Vancouver-																		
Hillsboro, OR-																		
WA	581	22,716	54,429	62,793	35,803	60,689	21,274	36,559	58,778	132,516	50,846	167,700	60,128	275,651	221,758	197,850	42,448	182,175

MSA	1994	1995	1996	1997	1998	1999	2000	2001	2002	2003	2004	2005	2006	2007	2008	2009	2010	2011
Sacramento -																		
Arden-Arcade-																		
Roseville, CA	10,717	0	1,386	0	17,029	63,913	0	206,922	175,913	363,087	296,622	71,267	208,880	221,769	257,972	136,910	76,619	116,336
San Antonio-																		
New																		
Braunfels, TX	14,598	48,793	2,416	1,131	12,522	42,036	14,618	82,959	77,081	82,143	62,554	71,098	113,136	270,253	316,262	174,258	168,043	290,701
Total	$653,399	$1,099,101	$1,708,935	$1,813,629	$3,194,434	$6,657,354	$5,034,980	$8,031,447	$9,676,461	$14,233,830	$9,918,313	$7,991,464	$9,027,830	$15,281,594	$16,813,086	$13,429,231	$10,159,674	$12,866,994

Source: GAO analysis of Freddie Mac data.

Note: All dollar figures are in 2012 dollars.

APPENDIX III: ADDITIONAL DATA ON FANNIE MAE AND FREDDIE MAC'S MULTIFAMILY ACTIVITIES

In this appendix, we present additional analyses of loan-level data and aggregated data provided by Fannie Mae and Freddie Mac. Specifically, we analyzed multifamily loan-level data for 1994 through 2011 from both enterprises to determine (1) the unpaid principal balance of loans purchased in each state and (2) the delinquency rates of loans with various debt-service coverage and loan-to-value (LTV) ratios. In addition, we asked both enterprises to provide aggregated multifamily data on their administrative costs.

Multifamily Loan Purchases by State

Table 14 contains data on the unpaid principal balance of multifamily loans Fannie Mae and Freddie Mac acquired in the 50 states, the District of Columbia, Puerto Rico, and the U.S. Virgin Islands from 1994 through 2011.

Table 14. Fannie Mae and Freddie Mac Multifamily Loan Acquisitions by State, 1994-2011

State	Fannie Mae (dollars in millions)	Fannie Mae rank	Freddie Mac (dollars in millions)	Freddie Mac rank
Alabama	$1,988	28	$1,910	23
Alaska	240	46	0	51
Arizona	6,866	12	4,672	14
Arkansas	796	38	484	37
California	97,281	1	47,630	1
Colorado	6,445	13	5,267	13
Connecticut	1,790	29	1,759	25
Delaware	966	36	347	41
District of Columbia	2,100	27	1,749	26
Florida	15,397	4	13,580	4
Georgia	7,307	10	10,105	6
Hawaii	734	40	361	39
Idaho	412	43	111	45
Illinois	7,652	9	6,775	8

State	Fannie Mae (dollars in millions)	Fannie Mae rank	Freddie Mac (dollars in millions)	Freddie Mac rank
Indiana	2,644	24	1,659	28
Iowa	761	39	467	38
Kansas	1,486	32	1,684	27
Kentucky	1,044	35	833	33
Louisiana	2,932	22	1,378	29
Maine	230	47	97	46
Maryland	11,039	6	9,966	7
Massachusetts	4,933	17	3,647	15
Michigan	5,362	15	2,370	20
Minnesota	4,035	20	3,017	17
Mississippi	722	41	706	36
Missouri	2,754	23	2,079	21
Montana	269	45	60	48
Nebraska	1,045	34	1,076	30
Nevada	5,943	14	2,915	19
New Hampshire	806	37	338	42
New Jersey	7,228	11	5,886	10
New Mexico	1,115	33	723	35
New York	40,653	2	17,923	3
North Carolina	4,897	18	5,713	11
North Dakota	219	48	272	43
Ohio	5,302	16	3,506	16
Oklahoma	2,275	26	812	34
Oregon	4,446	19	1,887	24
Pennsylvania	7,869	8	5,379	12
Puerto Rico	10	53	0	52
Rhode Island	480	42	360	40
South Carolina	1,695	30	1,995	22
South Dakota	280	44	126	44
Tennessee	3,178	21	2,916	18
Texas	24,748	3	22,462	2
Utah	2,308	25	970	32
Vermont	41	51	7	50
Virginia	8,179	7	10,928	5
Virgin Islands	13	52	0	53

Table 14. (Continued)

State	Fannie Mae (dollars in millions)	Fannie Mae rank	Freddie Mac (dollars in millions)	Freddie Mac rank
Washington	12,298	5	6,517	9
West Virginia	100	50	94	47
Wisconsin	1,625	31	1,064	31
Wyoming	130	49	31	49

Source: GAO analysis of data from Fannie Mae and Freddie Mac.

Note: All dollar figures are in 2012 dollars. For Fannie Mae, we included only those purchases where a single loan was associated with a single property, or about 99 percent of the loans Fannie Mae acquired during the period reviewed and about 85 percent of the unpaid principal balance.

Serious Delinquency Rates for Multifamily Loans with Various Underwriting Characteristics

Serious delinquency rates for multifamily loans varied by underwriting characteristic.

Table 15 contains loan counts and serious delinquency rates (based on unpaid principal balance) for multifamily loans with original debt-service coverage ratios less than 1.25 purchased from 1994 through 2011.

Table 15. Fannie Mae and Freddie Mac's Serious Delinquency Rates for Multifamily Loans with Debt-Service Coverage Ratios Less Than 1.25

	Fannie Mae		Freddie Mac	
Year	Number of multifamily loans with debt-service coverage ratios less than 1.25	Percentage of multifamily unpaid principal balance with debt-service coverage ratios less than 1.25 that was 60 days or more delinquent	Number of multifamily loans with debt-service coverage ratios less than 1.25	Percentage of multifamily unpaid principal balance with debt-service coverage ratios less than 1.25 that was 60 days or more delinquent
1994	N/A	N/A	15	0.00%
1995	373	0.00	25	0.00
1996	118	0.00	31	0.00

	Fannie Mae		Freddie Mac	
Year	Number of multifamily loans with debt-service coverage ratios less than 1.25	Percentage of multifamily unpaid principal balance with debt-service coverage ratios less than 1.25 that was 60 days or more delinquent	Number of multifamily loans with debt-service coverage ratios less than 1.25	Percentage of multifamily unpaid principal balance with debt-service coverage ratios less than 1.25 that was 60 days or more delinquent
1997	200	0.00	35	0.00
1998	878	0.09	36	0.00
1999	936	0.12	48	0.00
2000	1,033	0.00	55	0.00
2001	1,131	0.52	62	0.00
2002	1,420	0.01	195	0.00
2003	1,568	0.50	193	0.00
2004	1,829	0.21	244	0.00
2005	2,658	0.10	340	0.00
2006	3,231	0.07	436	0.00
2007	10,459	0.06	908	0.00
2008	11,367	0.29	1,294	0.08
2009	11,200	0.82	1,400	0.82
2010	10,710	0.77	1,421	0.82
2011	10,019	0.82	1,405	0.76

Source: GAO analysis of data from Fannie Mae and Freddie Mac.

N/A = not applicable.

Note: Fannie Mae's underwriting standards for traditional rental housing loans typically require a debt-service coverage ratio of 1.25. However, for certain asset classes, the ratio may be less than 1.25.

Table 16 contains loan counts and delinquency rates (based on unpaid principal balance) for multifamily loans with original debt-service coverage ratios greater than or equal to 1.25 purchased from 1994 through 2011.

Table 16. Fannie Mae and Freddie Mac's Serious Delinquency Rates for Multifamily Loans with Debt-Service Coverage Ratios Greater Than or Equal to 1.25

	Fannie Mae		Freddie Mac	
Year	Number of multifamily loans with debt-service coverage ratios greater than or equal to 1.25	Percentage of multifamily unpaid principal balance with debt-service coverage ratios greater than or equal to 1.25 that was 60 days or more delinquent	Number of multifamily loans with debt-service coverage ratios greater than or equal to 1.25	Percentage of multifamily unpaid principal balance with debt-service coverage ratios greater than or equal to 1.25 that was 60 days or more delinquent
1994	N/A	N/A	107	0.00%
1995	628	0.00	329	0.00
1996	1,106	0.09	700	0.04
1997	2,102	0.12	1,015	0.00
1998	4,921	0.04	1,585	0.00
1999	6,071	0.01	2,232	0.09
2000	6,900	0.08	2,647	0.00
2001	9,216	0.29	3,318	0.19
2002	16,336	0.05	4,408	0.14
2003	32,114	0.29	4,886	0.06
2004	31,499	0.10	5,244	0.08
2005	32,353	0.35	5,385	0.00
2006	24,893	0.08	5,397	0.06
2007	25,492	0.08	6,005	0.02
2008	28,034	0.30	6,914	0.02
2009	28,594	0.52	7,636	0.08
2010	28,804	0.67	8,110	0.17
2011	28,211	0.48	8,515	0.12

Source: GAO analysis of data from Fannie Mae and Freddie Mac.
N/A = not applicable.

Table 17 contains loan counts and delinquency rates (based on unpaid principal balance) for multifamily loans with original loan-to-value (LTV) ratios less than or equal to 80 percent purchased from 1994 through 2011.

Table 17. Fannie Mae and Freddie Mac's Serious Delinquency Rates for Multifamily Loans with LTV Ratios Less Than or Equal to 80 Percent

	Fannie Mae		Freddie Mac	
Year	Number of multifamily loans with LTV ratios less than or equal to 80 percent	Percentage of multifamily unpaid principal balance with LTV ratios less than or equal to 80 percent that was 60 days or more delinquent	Number of multifamily loans with LTV ratios less than or equal to 80 percent	Percentage of multifamily unpaid principal balance with LTV ratios less than or equal to 80 percent that was 60 days or more delinquent
1994	2	0.00%	122	0.00%
1995	974	0.00	355	0.00
1996	1,128	0.09	732	0.04
1997	2,122	0.12	1,048	0.00
1998	5,561	0.04	1,613	0.00
1999	6,613	0.01	2,262	0.09
2000	7,468	0.08	2,682	0.00
2001	9,773	0.30	3,355	0.19
2002	16,784	0.05	7,367	0.14
2003	32,353	0.28	17,547	0.01
2004	31,956	0.11	16,196	0.03
2005	35,103	0.32	14,432	0.00
2006	29,572	0.05	6,249	0.00
2007	34,506	0.06	7,066	0.02
2008	37,958	0.27	8,108	0.00
2009	38,369	0.62	8,876	0.10
2010	38,126	0.71	9,322	0.13
2011	36,885	0.49	9,680	0.10

Source: GAO analysis of data from Fannie Mae and Freddie Mac.

Table 18 contains loan counts and delinquency rates (based on unpaid principal balance) for multifamily loans with original LTV ratios greater than 80 percent purchased from 1994 through 2011.

Table 18. Fannie Mae and Freddie Mac's Serious Delinquency Rates for Multifamily Loans with LTV Ratios Greater Than 80 Percent

Fannie Mae			Freddie Mac	
Year	Number of multifamily loans with LTV ratios greater than 80 percent	Percentage of multifamily unpaid principal balance with LTV ratios greater than 80 percent that was 60 days or more delinquent	Number of multifamily loans with LTV ratios greater than 80 percent	Percentage of multifamily unpaid principal balance with LTV ratios greater than 80 percent that was 60 days or more delinquent
1994	0	0.00%	1	0.00%
1995	17	0.00	2	0.00
1996	53	0.00	2	0.00
1997	134	0.00	5	0.00
1998	485	0.00	11	0.00
1999	569	0.13	22	0.00
2000	686	0.00	23	0.00
2001	787	0.56	28	0.00
2002	1,078	0.00	271	0.00
2003	1,336	0.78	362	0.59
2004	1,335	0.21	421	0.61
2005	1,363	0.37	451	0.00
2006	1,327	0.44	387	0.91
2007	1,378	0.32	534	0.00
2008	1,383	0.89	698	0.46
2009	1,363	0.56	729	1.58
2010	1,328	0.56	754	2.36
2011	1,290	2.91	742	2.15

Source: GAO analysis of data from Fannie Mae and Freddie Mac.

Note: Fannie Mae's underwriting standards for traditional rental housing loans typically require an LTV ratio of 80 percent. However, for certain asset classes, the ratio may exceed 80 percent.

Multifamily Administrative Costs

The enterprises' administrative costs associated with their multifamily business from 2002 through 2011 are shown in table 19.

Table 19. Fannie Mae and Freddie Mac's Multifamily Administrative Costs, 2002- 2011

Year	Fannie Mae (dollars in millions)	Freddie Mac (dollars in millions)
2002	$192	No data
2003	236	No data
2004	270	No data
2005	424	$151
2006	597	182
2007	548	189
2008	404	190
2009	363	221
2010	383	212
2011	264	220

Sources: Fannie Mae and Freddie Mac.

Note: Fannie Mae could not provide data prior to 2002, and Freddie Mac could not provide data prior to 2005. For Fannie Mae, the data include direct expenses, direct allocated expenses, and indirect expenses for its entire multifamily business.

Appendix IV: Enterprises' Multifamily Loan and Property Sizes Compared with Other Market Participants

From 2005 through 2011, the size of the multifamily loans that Freddie Mac purchased and the properties it financed were more comparable with loans financed by life insurance companies than Fannie Mae. As shown in table 20, during this period Freddie Mac purchased loans and financed properties that were larger than those financed by Fannie Mae, generally comparable to those financed by life insurance companies, and generally larger than those financed by commercial mortgage-backed securities (CMBS) lenders. During the same period, Fannie Mae purchased smaller loans and financed smaller properties than those financed by Freddie Mac, life insurance companies, and CMBS lenders (except for 2010).

Table 20. Median Loan Size and Number of Units for Multifamily Loans Financed by the Enterprises, Life Insurance Companies, and CMBS Lenders, 2005-2011

Acquisition or origination year	Median loan size (dollars in thousands)				Median number of units			
	Fannie Mae	Freddie Mac	Life insurancecompanies	CMBS lenders	Fannie Maea	Freddie Mac	Life insurance companies	CMBS lenders
2005	$629	$7,450	$10,800	$5,400	13	196	210	144
2006	1,179	8,450	13,800	6,268	24	200	236	154
2007	691	7,768	13,840	7,200	15	192	224	144
2008	1,836	9,000	6,800	4,187	44	200	144	120
2009	3,280	10,170	4,850	b	92	217	144	b
2010	3,500	10,500	12,500	1,424	85	199	228	66
2011	4,365	11,500	13,000	9,040	102	212	207	222

Sources: GAO analysis of data from Fannie Mae and Freddie Mac; American Council of Life Insurers; and Trepp.

Note: For Fannie Mae and Freddie Mac, the year represents the year the loan was acquired. For life insurance companies and CMBS lenders, the year is the year the loan was originated.

[a] The numbers for Fannie Mae may be low because we excluded loans associated with multiple properties. Such loans tend to finance large properties, according to Fannie Mae.

[b] CMBS lenders did not originate any multifamily loans in 2009.

Other sources of multifamily housing financing—state and local housing finance agencies (HFA), loan consortiums, and the Rural Housing Service (RHS)—focused on smaller loans and properties for the most part.[1] For example, as shown in table 21, data for 2005 through 2011 from three state HFAs showed that they financed small loans (with median loan sizes ranging from more than $165,000 to about $4 million) and small properties (median units per property ranging from 12 to 95).

Three other state and local HFAs reported median loan sizes ranging from $3 million to $26 million and median units per property ranging from 76 to 230. RHS's average loan size ranged from about $1 million to $1.4 million.2 During this period, the median number of multifamily units supported by RHS ranged from 44 to 50.

Table 21. Median Loan Size and Number of Units for Loans Originated by Selected Housing Finance Agencies, 2005-2011

Origination year	Median loan size (dollars in thousands)							Median number of units				
	HFA 1	HFA 2	HFA 3	HFA 4	HFA 5	HFA 6	HFA 1	HFA 2	HFA3	HFA 4	HFA 5	HFA 6
2005	N/A	$4,472	$391	$165	$3,750	$11,523	N/A	175	58	18	70	125
2006	N/A	4,825	508	308	2,320	10,340	N/A	92	60	13	63	104
2007	$3,000	6,773	344	215	1,703	26,000	76	109	60	16	57	230
2008	8,150	5,695	3,081	200	2,350	8,530	106	102	95	14	80	78
2009	7,502	5,430	[a]	1,750	3,133	16,695	160	98	[a]	27	75	130
2010	7,345	4,680	790	1,500	N/A	10,620	101	105	40	16	N/A	107
2011	5,203	4,880	[a]	1,100	1,600	12,377	96	100	[a]	12	50	98

Sources: Selected housing finance agencies.
N/A = data not available
[a] HFA had no loans in 2009 and 2011.

The two loan consortiums that provided us with data reported much smaller loans than the enterprises, with median loan sizes ranging from $284,000 to $1.6 million and median number of units per property ranging from 12 to 43 (see table 22).

Table 22. Median Loan Size and Number of Units for Loans Originated by Selected Loan Consortiums, 2005-2011

Origination	Median loan size (dollars in thousands)		Median number of units	
year	LC 1	LC 2	LC 1	LC 2
2005	$284	$1,090	12	31
2006	421	865	18	18
2007	520	1,620	18	43
2008	625	1,480	21	35
2009	460	749	17	24
2010	343	745	15	40
2011	289	1,500	12	36

Sources: Selected loan consortiums.

APPENDIX V: DATA FROM SELECTED HOUSING FINANCE AGENCIES AND LOAN CONSORTIUMS

This appendix contains data provided by six state and local housing finance agencies (HFA) and three loan consortiums on the first-lien multifamily mortgages that they originated from 2005 through 2011. Specifically, they provided data on their median debt-service coverage ratios, median loan-to-value (LTV) ratios, and delinquency rates. These data are presented as examples of specific HFA and loan consortiums for the purposes of comparison against information provided in this report for each of the enterprises.

Because there can be variation between individual HFAs and individual loan consortiums, these data should not be seen as representative of all HFAs or loan consortiums.

Table 23 provides information on the median debt-service coverage and LTV ratios for loans originated by six HFAs from 2005 through 2011. The debt-service coverage ratio estimates a multifamily borrower's ability to service its mortgage obligation using the secured property's cash flow, after deducting nonmortgage expenses from income.

Table 23. Median Debt-Service Coverage and LTV Ratios for Loans Financed by Selected Housing Finance Agencies, 2005- 2011

	Median debt-service coverage ratio			*Median LTV ratio*		
Origination year	LC 1 LC 2		LC 3	LC 1 LC 2		LC 3
2005	1.24	1.27	1.17	80%	51%	N/A
2006	1.22	1.23	1.14	70	59	N/A
2007	1.21	1.17	1.13	71	38	N/A
2008	1.23	1.28	1.13	75	56	N/A
2009	1.24	1.31	1.15	76	47	N/A
2010	1.27	1.25	1.18	72	35	N/A
2011	1.31	1.49	1.20	70	46	N/A

Sources: Selected housing finance agencies.

N/A = data not available.

Note: The median LTV ratios for one of the HFAs are low because there are multiple sources of subordinate financing.

The higher the debt-service coverage ratio, the more likely a multifamily borrower will be able to continue servicing its mortgage obligation.

The LTV ratio is the ratio of the unpaid principal balance of a mortgage loan to the value of the property that serves as collateral for the loan, expressed as a percentage.

Loans with high LTV ratios generally tend to have a higher risk of default and, if a default occurs, a greater risk that the amount of the gross loss will be high compared to loans with lower LTV ratios.

Table 24 provides information on the median debt-service coverage and LTV ratios for loans originated by three loan consortiums from 2005 through 2011.

Table 24. Median Debt-Service Coverage Ratios and LTV Ratios for Loans Financed by Selected Loan Consortiums, 2005- 2011

	Median debt-service coverage ratio			*Median LTV ratio*		
Origination year	LC 1	LC 2	LC 3	LC 1	LC 2	LC 3
2005	1.24	1.27	1.17	80%	51%	N/A
2006	1.22	1.23	1.14	70	59	N/A
2007	1.21	1.17	1.13	71	38	N/A
2008	1.23	1.28	1.13	75	56	N/A
2009	1.24	1.31	1.15	76	47	N/A
2010	1.27	1.25	1.18	72	35	N/A
2011	1.31	1.49	1.20	70	46	N/A

Sources: Selected loan consortiums.
N/A = data not available.

Table 25 includes information on the percentage of loans seriously delinquent for the six HFAs.

The percentage of loans seriously delinquent (60 or more days delinquent) each year is based on unpaid principal balance and the status (as of December 2011) of only those loans originated in that year.

Table 26 includes information on the percentage of loans seriously delinquent for three loan consortiums.

Table 25. Percentage of Selected Housing Finance Agencies' Unpaid Principal Balances That Were Seriously Delinquent as of December 2011, 2005-2011

Origination		60 days or more delinquent				
year	HFA 1	HFA 2 HFA 3 HFA 4			HFA 5	HFA 6
2005	0.00%	0.00%	0.00%	0.00%	5.6%	0.00%
2006	0.00	0.00	0.00	0.00	7.1%	0.00
2007	0.00	0.00	0.00	0.00	0.0%	0.00
2008	0.00	0.00	0.00	0.00	0.0%	0.00
2009	0.00	0.00	0.00	0.00	0.0%	0.00
2010	0.00	0.00	0.00	0.00	N/A	0.00
2011	0.00	0.00	0.00	0.00	0.0%	0.00

Sources: Selected housing finance agencies.
N/A = data not available

Table 26. Percentage of Loans Seriously Delinquent for Selected Loan Consortiums, 2005-2011

	60 days or more delinquent		
Origination year	LC 1 LC 2		LC 3
2005	7.63%	0.00%	0.00%
2006	0.87	0.00	0.00
2007	0.00	0.00	0.00
2008	0.00	0.00	0.00
2009	0.00	0.00	0.00
2010	0.00	0.00	0.00
2011	0.00	0.00	0.00

Sources: Selected loan consortiums.

End Notes

[1] The Housing and Economic Recovery Act of 2008 (HERA), Pub. L. No. 110-289 (July 30, 2008), established FHFA, which is responsible for the safety and soundness and housing mission oversight of Fannie Mae, Freddie Mac, and the other housing government-sponsored enterprise, the Federal Home Loan Bank System.

[2] Congress initially chartered Fannie Mae in 1938 but did not establish it as a shareholder-owned corporation until 1968. Congress initially established Freddie Mac in 1970 as an entity within the Federal Home Loan Bank System and reestablished it as a shareholder-owned corporation in 1989.

[3] Conventional mortgages do not carry government insurance or guarantees and are the focus of this report.

[4] Each enterprise also holds some MBS in retained portfolio.

[5] Federal Housing Enterprises Financial Safety and Soundness Act of 1992 (Safety and Soundness Act), Pub. L. No. 102-550, title XIII. HERA transferred HUD's authorities and responsibilities for the goals to FHFA (§§ 1122, 1128). See 12 U.S.C. §§ 4561-4566.

[6] The Safety and Soundness Act required Fannie Mae and Freddie Mac each to meet specific numeric goals for the purchase of mortgages serving targeted groups each year. Specifically, it directed HUD to promulgate regulations setting goals for both enterprises targeted at borrowers or renters who (1) have low and moderate incomes, (2) live in underserved areas, and (3) have very low-income or have low-income and live in low-income areas (known as the special affordable housing goal).

[7] OFHEO was an independent agency in HUD responsible for the enterprises' safety and soundness. HERA created FHFA to oversee Fannie Mae and Freddie Mac and abolished OFHEO.

[8] Fannie Mae and Freddie Mac, the focus of this report, are secondary market institutions that purchase conventional loans and issue securities backed by those loans. Ginnie Mae guarantees the timely payment of principal and interest on securities issued by financial institutions and backed by pools of federally insured or guaranteed mortgage loans.

[9] Multifamily loans are made to borrowers under varying terms, but the balance is generally amortized over a term that is significantly longer than the life of the loan. As a result, there is little amortization of principal, resulting in a balloon payment at maturity.

[10] See Lawrence Goldberg and Charles A. Capone, Jr., "Multifamily Mortgage Credit Risk: Lessons from Recent History," Cityscape, 4, no. 1 (1998).

[11] The data on multifamily net charge-offs came from a Fannie Mae report prepared prior to its 2004 restatement of earnings.

[12] The data on multifamily net charge-offs came from a Freddie Mac report prepared prior to its 2003 restatement of earnings.

[13] In October 1991, we identified internal control weaknesses in Freddie Mac's multifamily program. We reported that in response to these weaknesses as well as to its financial losses, Freddie Mac suspended purchases in its major multifamily program. See GAO, Federal Home Loan Mortgage Corporation: Abuses in Multifamily Program Increase Exposure to Financial Losses, GAO/RCED-92-6 (Washington, D.C.: Oct. 7, 1991).

[14] As of July 2012, Fannie Mae had 25 approved DUS lenders.

[15] According to Freddie Mac officials, from 2005 through 2009 underwriting on a small segment of Freddie Mac's business, its targeted affordable loans, was performed by the targeted affordable seller/servicer on a delegated basis with risk shared by the seller/servicer and Freddie Mac. Targeted affordable loans include mortgages on properties subject to low-income housing tax credits, mortgages on properties that receive federal subsidies, and transactions in which Freddie Mac will credit enhance a mortgage that backs tax-exempt bonds, a trust certificate, or other instrument related to tax-exempt bonds.

[16] Under the K-deal program, which began in 2008, certain loans are sold to a third-party depositor that deposits the loans into a third-party trust. The third-party trust issues private-label securities backed by the loans. Freddie Mac purchases and guarantees certain bonds issued by the third-party trust and securitizes these bonds through a Freddie Mac trust. The resulting certificates guaranteed by Freddie Mac are publicly offered. The third-party trust issues unguaranteed subordinate bonds that are privately offered to investors.

[17] FHFA, on behalf of the enterprises, entered into separate Senior Preferred Stock Purchase Agreements with Treasury on September 7, 2008. The purchase agreements prevented the loss of capital at the enterprises through a purchase of up to $100 billion of senior preferred

stock in each enterprise as necessary to avoid a negative net worth. In 2009, Treasury amended the agreements to increase the amount of support for each enterprise to the greater of (1) $200 billion or (2) $200 billion plus the cumulative total of deficiency amounts determined for calendar quarters in 2010, 2011, and 2012, less any surplus amount determined as of December 31, 2012. In exchange for this support, the purchase agreements, as amended, required the mortgage asset portfolios of the enterprises to shrink by at least 10 percent (of the maximum amount they were permitted to hold at the end of the previous calendar year) every year until each enterprise's holdings of mortgages reached a balance of $250 billion. Another amendment to the agreements in August 2012 changed the amount to 15 percent. This included both single- and multifamily mortgages.

[18] Unpaid principal balance is the remaining outstanding balance on loans acquired and is a key metric the multifamily industry uses to measure portfolio activity.

[19] The enterprises' multifamily portfolios also include various types of credit enhancements for tax-exempt bonds issued by state and local HFAs to finance affordable rental housing. Should the bonds default, the enterprises guarantee that they will provide supplemental funds to permit the continued payment of principal and interest to bondholders. The mortgages associated with these credit enhancements were included in the loan-level data provided by both enterprises.

[20] Freddie Mac piloted K-deals in 2006.

[21] Specifically, in calculating goal performance each goal-qualifying unit financed in a 5 to 50 unit property counted as two units in the numerator, and one unit in the denominator.

[22] The Office of Management and Budget defines MSAs for use by federal statistical agencies in collecting, tabulating, and publishing statistics. They contain a core urban area with a population of 50,000 or more.

[23] Traditional multifamily rental housing is housing with five or more units that is not student, senior, manufactured, or cooperative housing. Multifamily loans for student housing are secured by properties in which college or graduate students make up at least 80 percent of the tenants, among other requirements. Multifamily loans for senior housing are secured by properties intended to be for residents aged 55 or older and that provide additional services for residents, such as group meals. Multifamily loans for manufactured housing are secured by a residential development that consists of sites for manufactured homes and includes infrastructure. A cooperative loan is a multifamily loan made to a cooperative housing corporation and secured by a first or second subordinate lien on a cooperative multifamily housing project that contains five or more units.

[24] According to Freddie Mac officials, they tend to report on their multifamily purchases as either traditional rental housing loans or targeted affordable loans. Targeted affordable loans include mortgages on properties subject to low-income housing tax credits, mortgages on properties that receive federal subsidies, and transactions in which Freddie Mac will credit enhance a mortgage that backs tax-exempt bonds, a trust certificate, or other instrument related to tax-exempt bonds.

[25] Fannie Mae's multifamily transactions involving multiple loans and multiple properties may be characterized by cross-collateralized and cross-defaulted loans. Crosscollateralization uses multiple properties to secure one loan. When such loans are also cross-defaulted, a default on one loan triggers default on the rest. Similar transactions undertaken by Freddie Mac are also characterized by a pool of cross-collateralized and cross-defaulted loans.

[26] Fannie Mae and Freddie Mac classify multifamily loans as seriously delinquent when payment is 60 days or more past due. Our analyses of delinquency rates are based on the unpaid principal balance of outstanding loans at the end of each year. Later in this report, we

present the delinquency rates for loans acquired or guaranteed in particular years and compare the enterprises' delinquency rates with those of other major market participants.

[27] As shown later in this report, Fannie Mae's serious delinquency rates for multifamily loans acquired in 2005 through 2010 were highest for 2007 and 2008. During the same period, Freddie Mac's serious delinquency rates were highest in 2006 and 2007.

[28] For Freddie Mac, we also discuss gain on sales of mortgages.

[29] For example, Fannie Mae's net income figures do not include net income from its capital markets division, which buys and sells multifamily and single-family MBS. Freddie Mac's net income figures are for its entire multifamily business.

[30] LIHTC is the primary program for the creation and preservation of rental housing that is affordable for low- and very low-income households. In February 2010, FHFA determined that the sale of any LIHTC investments made by the enterprises would require the consent of Treasury under the terms of the preferred stock purchase agreements. After FHFA consulted with Treasury, it decided that the enterprises could not sell or transfer the assets and required them to write down the value of the LIHTC investments to zero, causing substantial losses for the enterprises. This decision was reflected in the 2009 year-end financial statements, which were published in March 2010.

[31] Fannie Mae and Freddie Mac define net multifamily charge-offs as the realization of losses on loans that have been deemed uncollectible, typically due to foreclosure.

[32] Ninety-nine firms participated in MBA's 2011 origination survey, including life insurance companies, conduits for CMBS, lenders that sell loans to Fannie Mae and Freddie Mac, FHA lenders, and other lender groups. The survey did not include small banks and thrifts because they tend to operate as a separate market, according to MBA. Although not comprehensive, the survey data from MBA are the data most often cited when discussing the enterprises' share of the multifamily housing financing marketplace.

[33] Trepp is a provider of CMBS analytics, data, consulting, and software to the securities and investment management industry.

[34] To a lesser extent, the literature also noted that Fannie Mae and Freddie Mac have helped set underwriting standards in the multifamily market.

[35] See Mortgage Finance Working Group's Multifamily Subcommittee, Center for American Progress, A Responsible Market for Rental Housing Finance: Envisioning the Future of the U.S. Secondary Market for Multifamily Residential Rental Mortgages (October 2010); Denise DiPasquale, "Rental Housing: Current Market Conditions and the Role of Federal Policy," Cityscape, 13, no. 2 (2011); Ingrid Gould Ellen, John Napier Tye, and Mark A. Willis, Improving U.S. Housing Finance through Reform of Fannie Mae and Freddie Mac: Assessing the Options (NYU Furman Center for Real Estate and Urban Policy: May 2010); Joint Center for Housing Studies, Harvard University, Meeting Multifamily Housing Finance Needs During and After the Credit Crisis (2009); and Ethan Handelman, David A. Smith, and Todd Trehubenko, Government-Sponsored Enterprises and Multifamily Housing Finance: Refocusing on Core Functions, report prepared for the National Housing Conference (October 2010).

[36] Joint Center for Housing Studies, Harvard University, Meeting Multifamily Housing Finance Needs During and After the Credit Crisis (2009).

[37] Mortgage Finance Working Group's Multifamily Subcommittee, Center for American Progress, A Responsible Market for Rental Housing Finance: Envisioning the Future of the U.S. Secondary Market for Multifamily Residential Rental Mortgages (October 2010).

[38] Mortgage Finance Working Group's Multifamily Subcommittee, Center for American Progress, A Responsible Market for Rental Housing Finance: Envisioning the Future of the U.S. Secondary Market for Multifamily Residential Rental Mortgages (October 2010).

[39] While the American Community Survey reports on properties with 5 to 49 units as small, FHFA and the enterprises define small multifamily loans as those financing properties with 5 to 50 units.

[40] Low-income rental units are those affordable to households with income below 80 percent of area median income. Very low-income rental units are those affordable to households with incomes below 50 percent of area median income.

[41] Tom White and Charlie Wilkins, No Federal Guaranty for Multifamily and Other Ideas for Multifamily Housing Finance Reform, paper presented at an American Enterprise Institute-hosted event entitled "A New Lease on Loans: Ideas for Multifamily Housing Reform" (Washington, D.C.: Nov. 16, 2011).

[42] Peter J. Wallison, Alex J. Pollock, and Edward J. Pinto, Taking the Government Out of Housing Finance: Principles for Reforming the Housing Finance Market, an American Enterprise Institute Policy White Paper (Mar. 24, 2011).

[43] According to FHFA officials, the focus of this initiative is single-family mortgages. Securitization for single-family mortgages has been more standardized than for multifamily mortgages, which also has employed a different process. For example, the typical multifamily MBS that Fannie Mae issues is backed by a single multifamily loan, while its single-family MBS are backed by numerous single-family loans.

[44] Federal Housing Enterprises Financial Safety and Soundness Act of 1992, Pub. L. No. 102-550, §§ 1331-1334.

[45] A similar definition, based on counties, was employed for high-minority areas in nonmetropolitan areas. The income definitions were revised over time. For example, for 2005 through 2008 HUD revised the underserved areas goal to target households residing in (1) census tracts with median income at or below 80 percent of AMI in metropolitan areas, or (2) high-minority areas with tract median income at no more than 100 percent of AMI.

[46] According to a November 2010 paper by John C. Weicher (former Assistant Secretary for Housing at HUD from 2001 through 2005), the goals that HUD set did not ask the enterprises to lead the market; rather, the targets were consistently set so that they could be met. See Weicher, The Affordable Housing Goals, Homeownership and Risk: Some Lessons from Past Efforts to Regulate the GSEs, paper presented at a Federal Reserve Bank of St. Louis conference entitled "The Past, Present, and Future of the Government-Sponsored Enterprises" (St. Louis, Mo.: Nov. 17, 2010).

[47] See Pub. L. No. 110-289, Sec. 1128 (12 U.S.C. 4561).

[48] See Section 1333(a)(4) of the Safety and Soundness Act, as amended by HERA (12 U.S.C. 4563(a)(4)).

[49] See 74 Fed. Reg. 39873 (Aug. 10, 2009).

[50] The new affordable housing goals include four single-family goals and one single-family subgoal as well as one multifamily goal and one multifamily subgoal.

[51] See 75 Fed. Reg. 55892 (September 14, 2010).

[52] See 77 Fed. Reg. 34263 (June 11, 2012) (proposed rule). 53See 12 U.S.C. §§ 4544, 4566.

[54] See 12 C.F.R. §§ 1282.62 and 1282.63. 55See 12 U.S.C. § 4566.

[56] See, for example, HUD, Office of Policy Development and Research, Summary of U.S. Housing Market Conditions (Washington, D.C.: Summer 1998). We relied on these reports to determine whether the enterprises met their goals in 1993 through 2000 because FHFA

was unable to provide official annual reports from HUD showing each year's goals and the enterprises' performance relative to their goals.

[57] According to FHFA officials, Freddie Mac, and to a lesser extent Fannie Mae, depended heavily on CMBS purchases to attain the special affordable multifamily subgoal from 2006 to 2008.

[58] To determine the enterprises' total business and multifamily business, we considered purchases of mortgages and mortgage-related securities (MBS and mortgage revenue bonds).

[59] These programs are in addition to the enterprises' sharing of risk with lenders and investors, as discussed previously in the background section of this report.

[60] We also obtained data on credit standards and loan performance from a small number of participants that provide multifamily affordable housing loans: state and local HFAs and nonprofit loan consortiums (funded by a pool of local banks and thrifts).

[61] Aggregate data on the credit standards of banks and thrifts and FHA and RHS lenders are not readily available.

[62] The debt-service coverage ratio is an indicator of future credit performance for multifamily loans; the ratio estimates a multifamily borrower's ability to service its mortgage obligation using the secured property's cash flow, after deducting nonmortgage expenses from income. The higher the ratio, the more likely a multifamily borrower will be able to continue servicing its mortgage obligation. The LTV ratio is the ratio of the unpaid principal amount of a mortgage loan to the value of the property that serves as collateral for the loan, expressed as a percentage. Loans with high LTV ratios generally tend to have a higher risk of default and, if a default occurs, a greater risk that the amount of the gross loss will be high compared to loans with lower LTV ratios.

[63] One of the HFAs in our sample did not provide data on debt-service coverage ratios. 64The third loan consortium in our sample did not provide data on median LTV ratios.

[65] According to Trepp, these high delinquency rates were mainly attributable to a few large loans in New York City involving rent-controlled properties and several large developers in other parts of the country that had cash flow problems that largely have been resolved. Additionally, CMBS lenders relaxed their credit standards before the financial crisis, according to Trepp.

[66] Loans that were 90 days or more delinquent include loans in nonaccrual status, which are nonperforming loans that are not generating the stated interest rate because of nonpayment from the borrower, typically due to financial difficulties.

[67] According to Freddie Mac officials, life insurance companies tend to actively sell loans before they become delinquent. We confirmed with an ACLI official that insurance companies actively manage their portfolios of commercial mortgages, which sometimes involves selling potential problem loans and delinquent mortgages in order to minimize losses.

[68] Affordable multifamily housing projects are those in which (1) 20 percent or more of the rental units are both rent-restricted and occupied by families whose incomes are 50 percent or less of AMI, with adjustments for household size, or (2) 40 percent (25 percent in New York City) or more of the rental units are both rent-restricted and occupied by families whose incomes are 60 percent or less of AMI, with adjustments for household size.

[69] According to Fannie Mae, the enterprise will decrease its standard debt-service coverage requirement by 5 basis points (for example, from 1.20 to 1.15) and increase its standard LTV ratio (for example, from 80 to 85 percent), thereby generating between 4 and 5 percent additional proceeds to cover some of the costs of the renovations or retrofitting.

[70] If the term of the loan is 10-15 years and there is no amortization reserve, the risk-sharing premium is 50 basis points (.50 percent).

[71] According to Fannie Mae officials, HUD has been considering changes that Fannie Mae suggested to the execution of this program that would make it more attractive to the owners of existing affordable multifamily properties.

[72] These annual examinations are required by Section 1317 of the Safety and Soundness Act as amended (12 U.S.C. § 4517). Credit risk arises from an obligor's failure to meet the term of any financial contract with the enterprise or other failure to fulfill a financial commitment. Credit risk is found in activities in which success depends on counterparty, issuer, or borrower performance. The risk arises any time enterprise funds are extended, committed, invested, or otherwise exposed through actual or implied contractual agreements.

[73] These annual reports are required by Section 1319B of the Safety and Soundness Act, as amended (12 U.S.C. § 4521).

[74] The supervisory rating in the conclusion letter describes how well risks are identified, measured, monitored, controlled, and managed. The rating uses the following terms: no or minimal concerns, limited concerns, significant concerns, and critical concerns.

[75] We reviewed OFHEO's annual reports to Congress from 1997 through 2008. OFHEO reported deficiencies in Fannie Mae's multifamily activities in 2006, 2007, and 2008. While OFHEO and FHFA's annual reports to Congress are public documents, the results of individual FHFA reviews are confidential. Therefore, we limit our discussions of the findings to a summary.

[76] The watch list is a list of high-risk loans that receives ongoing oversight by Freddie Mac. Freddie Mac has various criteria for placing a loan on the watch list, including low debt-service coverage ratios, high LTV ratios, and loans that have gone delinquent.

End Notes doe Appendix I

[1] Unpaid principal balance is the remaining outstanding balance on loans acquired and is a key metric the multifamily industry uses to measure portfolio activity.

[2] For example, Fannie Mae's discount mortgage-backed securities—which are short-term securities—roll over every 30, 60, or 90 days until the maturity date of the underlying loan. New loan numbers get assigned after each security rollover, but the issuance of the new security does not represent new financing.

[3] The enterprises' multifamily portfolios include various types of credit enhancements for tax-exempt bonds issued by state and local housing finance agencies to finance affordable rental housing. Should the bonds default, the enterprises guarantee that they will provide supplemental funds to permit the continued payment of principal and interest to bondholders.

[4] Participation certificates are securities that represent undivided beneficial ownership interests in, and receive payments from, pools of multifamily residential mortgages that are held in trust for investors. In a tax-exempt bond securitization, pools of unenhanced tax-exempt and taxable multifamily housing revenue bonds support fully guaranteed tax-exempt and taxable securities. K-deals are securities that are generally backed by pools of newly purchased mortgages underwritten by Freddie Mac.

[5] Metropolitan statistical areas are geographic entities the Office of Management and Budget defined for use by federal statistical agencies in collecting, tabulating, and publishing federal statistics. They contain a core urban area with a population of 50,000 or more.

[6] Financing options offered by Fannie Mae can result in one loan for multiple properties, multiple loans for multiple properties, or multiple loans for one property.

[7] Traditional multifamily rental housing is housing with five or more units that is not student, senior, manufactured, or cooperative housing. Multifamily loans for student housing are secured by properties in which college or graduate students make up at least 80 percent of the tenants, among other requirements. Multifamily loans for senior housing are secured by properties intended to be for residents aged 55 or older and that provide additional services for residents, such as group meals. Multifamily loans for manufactured housing are secured by a residential development that consists of sites for manufactured homes and includes infrastructure. A cooperative loan is a multifamily loan made to a cooperative housing corporation and secured by a first or second subordinate lien on a cooperative multifamily housing project that contains five or more units.

[8] At Fannie Mae, transactions can involve multiple properties financed by one loan, multiple properties financed by multiple loans, or one property financed by multiple loans. At Freddie Mac, transactions can involve multiple properties financed by one loan or one property financed by multiple loans.

[9] Under the DUS model, Fannie Mae approves lenders and delegates to them the authority to underwrite, close, and sell loans to the enterprise without its prior review.

[10] The number of loans with missing values generally represented less than 5 percent of each enterprise's unpaid principal balance.

[11] When reporting delinquency rates, Fannie Mae typically divides the delinquent unpaid principal balance by the total outstanding unpaid principal balance. Because we did not have data on the delinquent unpaid principal, we used the current unpaid principal balance.

[12] The number of loans with missing values generally represented less than 5 percent of each enterprise's unpaid principal balance.

[13] Fannie Mae and Freddie Mac define net multifamily charge-offs as the realization of losses on loans that have been deemed uncollectible, typically due to foreclosure.

[14] Aggregate data for earlier years were not available. We also requested aggregated data on capital costs, capital reserves, and loan servicing fees, but the enterprises were not able to provide data specific to their multifamily business.

[15] We reviewed data for 2005 through 2011 so that we could determine the enterprises' share of the multifamily housing financing marketplace before and after the financial crisis of 2007.

[16] Board of Governors of the Federal Reserve System, Flow of Funds Accounts of the United States, Z.1 Statistical Release, Table L.219 (June 7, 2012).

[17] Trepp is a provider of CMBS analytics, data, consulting, and software to the securities and investment management industry.

[18] See Mortgage Finance Working Group's Multifamily Subcommittee, Center for American Progress, A Responsible Market for Rental Housing Finance: Envisioning the Future of the U.S. Secondary Market for Multifamily Residential Rental Mortgages (October 2010); Denise DiPasquale, "Rental Housing: Current Market Conditions and the Role of Federal Policy," Cityscape, 13, no. 2 (2011); Ingrid Gould Ellen, John Napier Tye, and Mark A. Willis, Improving U.S. Housing Finance through Reform of Fannie Mae and Freddie Mac: Assessing the Options (NYU Furman Center for Real Estate and Urban Policy: May 2010); Joint Center for Housing Studies, Harvard University, Meeting Multifamily Housing Finance Needs During and After the Credit Crisis (2009); Ethan Handelman, David A. Smith, and Todd Trehubenko, Government-Sponsored Enterprises and Multifamily Housing Finance: Refocusing on Core Functions, report prepared for the National Housing Conference (October 2010); Peter J. Wallison, Alex J. Pollock, and Edward J. Pinto, Taking

the Government Out of Housing Finance: Principles for Reforming the Housing Finance Market, an American Enterprise Institute Policy White Paper (Mar. 24, 2011); and Tom White and Charlie Wilkins, No Federal Guaranty for Multifamily and Other Ideas for Multifamily Housing Finance Reform, paper presented at an American Enterprise Institute-hosted event entitled "A New Lease on Loans: Ideas for Multifamily Housing Reform" (Washington, D.C.: Nov. 16, 2011).

[19] See, for example, John C. Weicher, The Affordable Housing Goals, Homeownership and Risk: Some Lessons from Past Efforts to Regulate the GSEs, paper presented at a Federal Reserve Bank of St. Louis conference entitled "The Past, Present, and Future of the Government-Sponsored Enterprises" (St. Louis, Mo.: Nov. 17, 2010).

[20] See, for example, HUD, Office of Policy Development and Research, Summary of U.S. Housing Market Conditions (Washington, D.C.: Summer 1998). We relied on these reports to determine whether the enterprises met their goals in 1993 through 2000 because FHFA was unable to provide official annual reports from HUD showing each year's goals and the enterprises' performance relative to their goals.

[21] According to NCSHA officials, they recommended these state and local HFAs based on the large size of their multifamily programs and because they provided diversity in geography and size.

[22] One HFA was unable to provide us with median debt-service coverage ratios. 23These were the only three consortiums that responded to our request for data.

[24] One loan consortium was unable to provide us with data on median LTV ratios, median loan sizes, and median number of units per property.

End Note for Appendix II

[1] Metropolitan statistical areas are geographic entities the Office of Management and Budget defined for use by federal statistical agencies in collecting, tabulating, and publishing federal statistics. They contain a core urban area with a population of 50,000 or more.

End Note for Appendix IV

[1] The Federal Housing Administration was not able to provide data on average or median loan and property size.

[2] RHS was only able to provide us with average loan size.

In: Multifamily Housing
Editor: Jacob A. Pezzo

ISBN: 978-1-62417-654-8

Chapter 2

FANNIE MAE'S AND FREDDIE MAC'S FINANCIAL STATUS: FREQUENTLY ASKED QUESTIONS*

N. Eric Weiss

SUMMARY

Fannie Mae and Freddie Mac are charted by Congress as government-sponsored enterprises (GSEs) to provide liquidity in the mortgage market and promote homeownership for underserved groups and locations. They purchase mortgages, guarantee them, and package them in mortgage-backed securities (MBSs), which they either keep as investments or sell to institutional investors. In addition to the GSEs' guarantees, investors widely believe that MBSs are implicitly guaranteed by the federal government. In 2008, the GSEs financial condition had weakened and there were concerns over their ability to meet their obligations on \$1.2 trillion in bonds and \$3.7 trillion in MBSs that they had guaranteed. In response to the financial risks, the federal government took control of these GSEs in a process known as conservatorship as a means to stabilize the mortgage credit market.

Congressional interest in Fannie Mae and Freddie Mac has increased in recent years, primarily because the federal government's continuing

* This is an edited, reformatted and augmented version of a Congressional Research Service publication, CRS Report for Congress R42760, from www.crs.gov, prepared for Members and Committees of Congress, dated September 27, 2012.

conservatorship of these GSEs, at a time of uncertainty in the housing, mortgage, and financial markets, has raised doubts about the future of the enterprises and the potential cost to the Treasury of guaranteeing the enterprises' debt. Since more than 60% of households are homeowners, a large number of citizens could be affected by the future of the GSEs. Congress exercises oversight over the Federal Housing Finance Agency (FHFA), which is both regulator and conservator of the GSEs, and is considering legislation to shape the future of the GSEs.

Estimates of the eventual total cost to the federal government of supporting the GSEs use different baselines and vary widely. FHFA estimates that Treasury is likely to purchase $220 billion-$311 billion of senior preferred stock by the end of 2014. The Congressional Budget Office estimates the budget cost to be more than $300 billion. Standard & Poor's has estimated the cost at $280 billion plus $405 billion to create a replacement system.

Under terms of the federal government's support agreement as amended and effective on August 17, 2012, the enterprises will pay the Treasury all of their quarterly profits (if any). Under the previous agreements, the enterprises paid Treasury dividends of nearly $20 billion annually (10% of the support). Paying the federal government all profits earned in a quarter could prevent the GSEs from accumulating funds to redeem the senior preferred stock. However, it would appear that the GSEs could make quarterly redemptions.

The financial condition of the GSEs appears to be improving. In the first and second quarters of 2012, both Fannie Mae and Freddie Mac reported profits for the first time since the fourth quarter of 2006. Also, the second quarter of 2012 was first time that neither GSE had to request financial support from the Treasury.

INTRODUCTION

Fannie Mae and Freddie Mac are stockholder-owned, government-sponsored enterprises (GSEs), which purchase existing mortgages, guarantee investors that the mortgages will be paid on time, pool the mortgages into mortgage-backed securities (MBSs), and either keep the MBSs as an investment or sell the MBSs to investors. Congressional charters give the GSEs a special relationship with the federal government, and it is widely believed that the federal government implicitly guarantees their $1.2 trillion in bonds and $3.7 trillion in MBSs. The charters give these GSEs special public policy goals aimed at providing liquidity in the mortgage market and promoting homeownership for underserved groups and locations.

In 2008, the GSEs financial condition had weakened and there were concerns over their ability to meet obligations. On September 7, 2008, the federal government took control of these GSEs from their stockholders and management in a process known as conservatorship. The goal of conservatorship is to restore the GSEs' financial strength and to return control to their stockholders and management. Congressional interest in Fannie Mae and Freddie Mac has increased in recent years, primarily because the federal government's continuing conservatorship of these GSEs has raised doubts about their future and concerns about the potential cost of supporting them. Congressional interest has been reflected by the introduction of bills to reform or replace the GSEs and by oversight hearings.

This report presents, in analytical question and answer form, the major issues surrounding Fannie Mae's and Freddie Mac's financial conditions, and various public policy options under discussion.

A glossary of terms is included at the end of this report.

A Brief History of Fannie Mae and Freddie Mac

Prior to the development of the secondary mortgage market, mortgage markets were local, and there were significant differences across the nation in mortgage rates and relatively large fluctuations in lending activity. Primary lenders had to balance their lending practices with their deposits received, which led to severe credit shortages during economic downturns, when savings accounts were depleted by withdrawals.[1] This shortage was exacerbated due to the concentration of major money centers in areas like Chicago and New York, far from many who needed home loans. There was no way to move funds from these areas where mortgage money was available to other areas, such as California, where it was in relatively short supply. In effect, this amounted to a geographic barrier that prevented the law of supply and demand from operating on a national level in the home loan market.[2] The secondary mortgage market combined these many regional mortgage markets into a single national market that draws financing from around the world.

To encourage improvement in housing standards and conditions and to provide a system of mutual mortgage insurance, Congress passed, and President Franklin D. Roosevelt signed into law, the National Housing Act in 1934.[3] Title III of the National Housing Act established national mortgage associations, giving rise to the creation of Fannie Mae. In its original form, Fannie Mae was a federal government agency that was chartered to support government-backed mortgages and carry out some government subsidy functions. In 1954, Congress re-chartered Fannie Mae as a mixed government and private-sector entity, with a clearly delineated separation between its market-oriented (i.e., secondary mortgage trading) and governmental (i.e., special assistance and managing and liquidating government-held mortgages) functions.[4] In 1968, Congress split the firm into two distinct organizations, with the secondary market arm retaining the Fannie Mae name and the government functions arm taking the name Ginnie Mae, short for the Government National Mortgage Association.[5] The partitioning legislation re-chartered Fannie Mae as a GSE to become completely privately owned with no federal funding. Fannie Mae completed this transition in 1970.

In 1970, Congress enacted the Emergency Home Finance Act,[6] which authorized Fannie Mae to buy conventional mortgages. Fannie Mae bought most of the mortgages from mortgage bankers. Savings and loans, the other major source of mortgage money, were restricted to holding mortgages and were generally unable to work with Fannie Mae. To facilitate secondary market trading of conventional mortgages for savings and loan associations, the act created Freddie Mac as a wholly owned subsidiary of the Federal Home Loan Bank System (FHLBS). In 1989, Congress re-chartered Freddie Mac so that its shares could trade on the New York Stock Exchange, in the same manner as Fannie Mae's.[7] The 1989 act also did away with the separate missions of Fannie Mae and Freddie Mac, with the result that today the two enterprises have similar characteristics.

Fannie Mae and Freddie Mac purchase mortgages that lenders have already made to homeowners. These mortgages must meet Fannie Mae's and Freddie Mac's standards and not exceed the conforming loan limit.[8] These mortgages are guaranteed by the purchasing GSE, pooled into MBSs, and either sold to investors or kept by the GSE as an investment.

FANNIE MAE'S AND FREDDIE MAC'S CURRENT STATUS

What Is the Current Financial Condition of Fannie Mae and Freddie Mac?

In the second quarter of 2012, Fannie Mae and Freddie Mac both reported profits. *Table 1* summarizes the losses and profits of Fannie Mae and Freddie Mac since 2006. Since 2007, neither GSE has reported a profitable year, but there have been profitable quarters.

Table 1. GSE Profitability Since 2006
($ in millions)

Quarter	Fannie Mae	Freddie Mac
1st Quarter 2006	$2,026	$1,942
2nd Quarter 2006	2,058	1,336
3rd Quarter 2006	-629	-550
4th Quarter 2006	604	401
Full Year 2006	*4,059*	*2,327*
1st Quarter 2007	961	-133
2nd Quarter 2007	1,947	729
3rd Quarter 2007	-1,399	-1,238
4th Quarter 2007	-3,559	-2,452
Full Year 2007	*-2,050*	*-3,094*
1st Quarter 2008	-2,186	-151
2nd Quarter 2008	-2,300	-821
3rd Quarter 2008	-28,994	-25,295
4th Quarter 2008	-25,227	-23,852
Full Year 2008	*-58,707*	*-50,119*
1st Quarter 2009	-23,168	-9,975
2nd Quarter 2009	-14,754	302
3rd Quarter 2009	-18,872	-5,408
4th Quarter 2009	-15,175	-6,472
Full Year 2009	*-71,969*	*-21,553*
1st Quarter 2010	-11,530	-6,688
2nd Quarter 2010	-1,218	-4,713
3rd Quarter 2010	-1,339	-2,511
4th Quarter 2010	73	-113
Full Year 2010	*-14,014*	*-14,025*
1st Quarter 2011	-6,471	676
2nd Quarter 2011	-2,893	-2,139
3rd Quarter 2011	-5,085	-4,422
4th Quarter 2011	-2,406	619
Full Year 2011	*-16,855*	*-5,266*
1st Quarter 2012	2,719	577
2nd Quarter 2012	4,114	3,020

Source: Fannie Mae (http://www.fanniemae.com/portal/about-us/investor-relations/index.html and Freddie Mac (http://www.freddiemac.com/investors.

Notes: Freddie Mac's 2009 annual report revised previously released 2009 quarterly net income. This table reflects the revisions. Amounts shown are "net loss attributable to Fannie Mae," and "net loss attributable to Freddie Mac," which exclude dividends paid to Treasury on the senior preferred stock. All other dividends have been suspended.

The second quarter of 2012 was also the first time that neither GSE had to request financial support from the Treasury (see *Table 2*).

The GSEs' losses that started in late 2006 are notable because, previously, the GSEs had been consistently profitable.

Prior to 2006, Fannie Mae had not reported a full-year loss since 1985, and Freddie Mac had never reported a full-year loss since it became stockholder owned.[9]

Two major sources of losses for mortgage lenders, [10] including the GSEs, have been loans to borrowers with less than prime credit (subprime) and certain types of mortgages to borrowers with credit between prime and subprime (Alt-A).[11]

At the end of 2011, Fannie Mae held $16.6 billion in private-label MBSs backed by subprime mortgages and held $19.7 billion in private-label MBSs backed by Alt-A mortgages.[12] Freddie Mac held $49.0 billion in private-label MBSs backed by subprime mortgages and $16.8 billion in private-label MBSs backed by Alt-A mortgages.[13]

The GSEs have, in addition, increased loan loss reserves in anticipation of continuing losses. If losses on foreclosed mortgages are less than predicted, the reserves could be reduced, which would improve the GSEs' financial condition. If losses are greater on foreclose mortgages, the GSEs' financial condition would worsen.

Starting in 2008, Fannie Mae and Freddie Mac have tightened their lending standards. For example, the average FICO score of a 2007 mortgage purchased by Freddie Mac was 703, in 2008 it was 722, and in 2012 it is 756.[14] Fannie Mae shows a similar increase in FICO scores. Approximately 64% of Fannie Mae's single-family book of business has been purchased in 2008 or more recently; the number for Freddie Mac is approximately 63%.

Since the third quarter of 2008, the Federal Housing Finance Agency (FHFA), as conservator of the GSEs, has asked Treasury for a total of $116.1 billion to increase Fannie Mae's assets to offset its liabilities, and a total of $71.3 billion for Freddie Mac.[15] The second quarter of 2012 was the first time that neither GSE required Treasury's support since the first draw in the third quarter of 2008.

Technically, Treasury support for the GSEs comes through purchases of GSE senior preferred stock. Table 2 reports the amounts, including the $1 billion of senior preferred stock that each GSE gave Treasury when they were taken into conservatorship.

This stock is senior to (has priority over) all other common and preferred stock; it is the only stock currently receiving dividends.

Table 2. Treasury Purchases of GSE Senior Preferred Stock ($ in millions)

	Fannie Mae	*Freddie Mac*
Initial Agreement (No explicit cost)	$1,000	$1,000
3rd Quarter 2008	0	13,800
4th Quarter 2008	15,200	30,800
Year 2008	*16,200*	*45,600*
1st Quarter 2009	19,000	6,100
2nd Quarter 2009	10,700	0
3rd Quarter 2009	15,000	0
4th Quarter 2009	15,300	0
Year 2009	*60,000*	*6,100*
1st Quarter 2010	8,400	10,600
2nd Quarter 2010	1,500	1,800
3rd Quarter 2010	2,500	100
4th Quarter 2010	2,600	500
Year 2010	*15,000*	*13,000*
1st Quarter 2011	8,500	0
2nd Quarter 2011	5,087	1,479
3rd Quarter 2011	7,791	5,992
4th Quarter 2011	4,571	146
Year 2011	*25,949*	*7,617*
1st Quarter 2012	0	19
2nd Quarter 2012	0	0
Total Holdings	*$117,149*	*$72,336*

Source: Fannie Mae (http://www.fanniemae.com/portal/about-us/investor-relations/index.html), Freddie Mac (http://www.freddiemac.com/investors and FHFA (http://www.fhfa.gov/Default.aspx?Page=70).

Note: Each "total holdings" includes $1 billion in senior preferred stock that the GSEs gave Treasury at the time of their conservatorship agreements. Except for the first draw, Treasury has actually paid the GSEs on the last day of the next quarter: March 31, June 30, September 30, and December 31.

In addition to Treasury's purchases of senior preferred stock, the Federal Reserve (Fed) has purchased GSE bonds and MBSs. In programs that started in September 2008 and ended in March 2010, the Fed and Treasury together purchased $1,135.9 billion in MBSs.16 On September 21, 2011, the Fed decided to begin reinvesting MBS principal repayments in other MBSs.17 As of the end of the second quarter of 2012, the Fed held $855.0 billion of Fannie Mae's and Freddie Mac's MBSs.[18]

How Do the GSEs Pay Dividends to Treasury?

To expedite reducing assets of the GSEs, Treasury, FHFA, and each of the GSEs amended the separate support contracts on August 17, 2012, so that each GSE pays Treasury whatever profits it earns each quarter.[19] If there are no profits, there is no payment. Previously each GSE made quarterly payments on a 10% dividend on the senior preferred stock.

Table 3. Dividends Paid by GSEs to Treasury ($ in billions)

		Fannie Mae			Freddie Mac		
Year	Quarter	Dividends Accrued	Date Paid	Cumulative Dividends	Dividends Accrued	Date Paid	Cumulative Dividends
2008	Q3	$0.01	N/A	$0.00	$0.01	N/A	$0.00
2008	Q4	$0.03	12/31/08	$0.03	$0.17	12/31/08	$0.17
2009	Q1	$0.03	3/31/09	$0.06	$0.37	3/31/09	$0.54
2009	Q2	$0.41	6/30/09	$0.47	$1.15	6/30/09	$1.69
2009	Q3	$0.89	9/30/09	$1.35	$1.29	9/30/09	$2.99
2009	Q4	$1.15	12/31/09	$2.50	$1.29	12/31/09	$4.28
2010	Q1	$1.53	3/31/10	$4.03	$1.29	3/31/10	$5.57
2010	Q2	$1.91	6/30/10	$5.94	$1.29	6/30/10	$6.86
2010	Q3	$2.12	9/30/10	$8.06	$1.56	9/30/10	$8.42
2010	Q4	$2.15	12/31/10	$10.21	$1.60	12/31/10	$10.03
2011	Q1	$2.22	3/31/11	$12.42	$1.61	3/31/11	$11.63
2011	Q2	$2.28	6/30/11	$14.71	$1.62	6/30/11	$13.25
2011	Q3	$2.50	9/30/11	$17.20	$1.62	9/30/11	$14.87
2011	Q4	$2.62	12/30/11	$19.82	$1.66	12/30/11	$16.52
2012	Q1	$2.82	3/30/12	$22.64	$1.81	3/30/12	$18.33
2012	Q2	$2.93	6/29/12	$25.57	$1.81	6/29/12	$20.14
Cumulative Dividends Paid by Both Enterprises $45.71 billion							

Source: FHFA, "Data as of August 8, 2012 on Treasury and Federal Reserve Purchase Programs for GSE and Mortgage-Related Securities," available at http://www.fhfa.gov/Default.aspx?Page=70.

Notes: Dividends accrued may not add up to cumulative dividends due to rounding.

What Risks Do Fannie Mae's and Freddie Mac's Financial Problems Create for Homeowners and Those Planning to Become Homeowners?

Fannie Mae's and Freddie Mac's financial problems create no risks for homeowners who want to stay in their homes and who do not want to refinance. Homeowners continue to pay their existing mortgages.

Treasury's actions of lending money to the GSEs and the Fed's purchases of the GSEs' MBSs appear to have helped stabilize the secondary mortgage market and provided a continuing flow of funds to purchase new homes and to refinance existing mortgages.

Under conservatorship, the GSEs have become active in loan modifications and the refinancing of existing mortgages that they own. They have raised the credit and documentation standards on the mortgages that they purchase, with stricter underwriting rules and higher fees. These actions are similar to other lenders' behavior during the recent recession and in previous economic slowdowns.

The Economic Stimulus Act of 2008 (ESA) raised the loan limit for FHA guaranteed loans in most high-cost areas of the nation to the same maximum that the GSEs are permitted to purchase.[20] As a result, FHA-guaranteed loans can, in theory, replace most conventional mortgages.

What Risks Do Fannie Mae and Freddie Mac Face in Today's Economic Environment?

In any economic environment, Fannie Mae and Freddie Mac face the variety of risks that many other companies face. The GSEs purchase home mortgages. They package most mortgages into MBSs, selling some and holding others in their investment portfolios. The GSEs finance their portfolios of long-term (typically 30-year) mortgages with short-term borrowing (typically three months to five years). This financing strategy increases the GSEs' profits because short-term borrowing is usually less expensive than longer term loans. At the same time, it creates *interest rate risk*, which is the risk that, if short-term interest rates increase, profitability can be reduced or can even turn to losses. For example, if interest rates were to increase to 6%, mortgages at 5% would not be profitable.[21] To try to reduce interest rate risk, the GSEs use a variety of financial derivatives.[22]

The Federal Reserve has said that it will hold interest rates low "at least through mid-2015"[23] and that it would attempt to lower longer-term interest rates.[24] In the short run, this could aid the GSEs: they finance mortgages by borrowing for relatively short periods of time and will be able to borrow at lower interest rates. In the longer run, when interest rates increase, the GSEs' profitability may be challenged as they refinance their short-term borrowing at rates that could be greater than what they receive on their mortgages.

In a worst-case scenario, the interest rate on short-term loans to the GSEs could increase enough to cause substantial losses, and investors could stop entering into derivative contracts with the GSEs. This would leave the GSEs, which anticipated being able to roll over their short-term debt, unable to refinance.

The GSEs are also subject to *credit risk*. The GSEs guarantee timely payment of principal and interest of the mortgages in their MBSs. As mortgage foreclosure rates have climbed since 2006, and as home prices have fallen, the value of the mortgages and MBSs that the two firms hold in their portfolio has also fallen. Uncertainty about the duration and severity of the housing slump means that markets cannot now gauge the riskiness of the GSEs with much confidence or precision. The Treasury's support has reduced this risk, but it is not clear if the GSEs will ever return to stockholder control.

Like all other businesses, the GSEs have *operational risk* due to the failure of internal controls. FHFA has directed the GSEs to reduce operational risk by improving their information technology, data quality, and internal controls.

As financial corporations, the GSEs are also subject to *model risk*, or the risk that their models (especially credit models) are not accurate. FHFA has directed the GSEs to update their financial models to reflect changing conditions.

What Is the Expected Cost to the Federal Government?

Estimates of the total cost to the federal government of supporting Fannie Mae and Freddie Mac use different baselines and vary widely.[25] FHFA has estimated that, by the end of 2014, Treasury is likely to have purchased $220 billion-$311 billion of senior preferred stock[26] and the Congressional Budget Office has estimated the budget cost "will exceed $300 billion....but the net effect on federal debt is likely to be smaller."[27]

Standard & Poor's has estimated that the total cost to resolve (wind down) the GSEs could be $280 billion, and that it would cost another $405 billion to capitalize (create) a new entity or entities to replace Fannie Mae and Freddie Mac.[28]

To keep the GSEs solvent from 2010 through 2012, Treasury has agreed to purchase as much senior preferred stock as necessary.[29] Treasury initially had agreed to purchase a maximum of $100 billion in senior preferred stock from each GSE, and later increased the $100 billion to $200 billion. After 2012, any unused portions of the $200 billion could still be used.[30] Treasury's authority to contract with the enterprises expired December 31, 2009.[31]

Upon entering conservatorship (September 7, 2008), each GSE issued Treasury $1 billion of senior preferred stock and warrants (options) to purchase common stock. If the warrants are exercised, Treasury would own 79.9% of each company. As part of the contracts, each GSE has agreed to restrictions on paying dividends, issuing new stock, and disposing of assets.

The agreements between the GSEs and Treasury set the maximum portfolio size for each GSE at $900 billion as of December 31, 2009, with the goal of reaching $250 billion by decreasing the maximum 10% annually. This 10% reduction applied in 2010 and 2012, but under the third amended agreement between Treasury and the GSEs, the maximum decreases 15% annually until it reaches $250 billion. Under the new, more rapid portfolio reductions, the $250 billion goal will be reached in 2018 instead of 2022. By way of reference, Fannie Mae's retained mortgage portfolio was $789 billion at the end of 2010 and $708 billion at the end of 2011. Freddie Mac's retained portfolio was $697 billion at the end of 2010 and $653 billion at the end of 2011.

The December 24, 2009, announcement said that Treasury would terminate its program to purchase MBSs of GSEs on December 31, 2009. Treasury estimated that the end of 2009 that it held approximately $220 billion in MBSs.[32] Treasury has said that it expects to profit from the spread between the interest rate that it pays to borrow money through bonds and the mortgage payments on the MBSs. Separately, the New York Federal Reserve had its own program to purchase $1.25 trillion of GSE and Ginnie Mae MBSs.[33] The Fed's new QE3 program is purchasing GSE and Ginnie Mae MBSs.[34] The GSEs will guarantee payment of the MBSs.

Treasury created a Government Sponsored Enterprise Credit Facility (GSECF) to provide liquidity to the GSEs, secured by MBSs pledged as collateral.35 This facility terminated December 31, 2009.

What Risks Do Fannie Mae and Freddie Mac Create for the U.S. Government?

In the event that it were necessary to dissolve Fannie Mae or Freddie Mac (a process known as receivership), the usual priority of claims on remaining assets is administrative expenses of the receivership, senior and general debt, subordinated debt, and stock.[36] This would seem to place the MBSs with their guarantee at a fairly senior position, followed by GSE bonds, which would be ahead of the government's senior preferred stock, which would be ahead of all other stockholders.

If a GSE were to go into receivership, the value of its MBSs could decline because the value of the guarantee of timely payment of the MBSs would be called into question. If a GSE were unable to perform on the timely payment guarantee, the value of the MBSs would depend on the payment of the underlying mortgages, the rules of receivership, and the government's support for the MBSs.

The eventual value of the bonds would depend on the cause of the receivership and the details of the liquidation process. For example, if mortgage defaults and losses were to increase, the assets available for creditors would decrease.

In the event of receivership, it would appear unlikely that the senior preferred stock would have much value.

Is the Government Investigating Fannie Mae and Freddie Mac?

The existence of an investigation is not usually announced or acknowledged, but there have been media reports that the Securities and Exchange Commission (SEC) is investigating several current or former GSE executives.[37]

SEC is reported to have sent formal notice of its intent to recommend civil charges against former Fannie Mae chief executive officer (CEO) Daniel H. Mudd, former Freddie Mac CEO Richard F. Syron, former Freddie Mac chief financial officer Anthony S. Piszel, and Freddie Mac executive vice president Donald J. Bisenius.

These notices (known as Wells notices) provide the opportunity to respond to the charges and to persuade the SEC not to proceed with the recommendation to the commission to file civil charges.

What Is Happening to Fannie Mae's and Freddie Mac's Affordable Housing Initiatives?

The Housing and Economic Recovery Act of 2008 (HERA; P.L. 110-289) gives the FHFA authority to set housing goals for Fannie Mae and Freddie Mac.

Table 4 summarizes the 2010 to 2014 housing goals and subgoals. Fannie Mae and Freddie Mac can also meet a housing goal or subgoal by purchasing sufficient qualifying mortgages to mirror or exceed the market.[38]

Table 4. GSE 2010-2014 Housing Goals and Subgoals

Category	2010-2011 Actual Goal	2012-1014 Proposed Goal
Low-Income Families Housing Goal (Fannie Mae, Freddie Mac)	27% purchase money(mortgages used to purchase a home)	20% purchase money
Very Low-Income Families Housing Goal (Fannie Mae, Freddie Mac)	8% purchase money	7% purchase money
Low-Income Areas Housing Goal (Fannie Mae, Freddie Mac)	13% purchase money	11% purchase money
Refinancing Housing Goal (Fannie Mae, Freddie Mac)	21% refinance	21% refinance
Multifamily Low-Income Housing Goal (Fannie Mae)	177,750 dwelling units	2012: 251,000 dwelling units 2013: 245,000 dwelling units 2014: 223,000 dwelling units
Multifamily Low-Income Housing Goal (Freddie Mac)	161,250 dwelling units	2012: 191,000 dwelling units 2013: 203,000 dwelling units 2014: 181,000 dwelling units
Multifamily Very Low-Income Housing Subgoal (Fannie Mae)	42,750 dwelling units	2012: 60,000 dwelling units 2013: 59,000 dwelling units 2014: 53,000 dwelling units
Multifamily Very Low-Income Housing Subgoal (Freddie Mac)	21,000 dwelling units	2012: 32,000 dwelling units 2013: 31,000 dwelling units 2014: 27,000 dwelling units

Sources: Federal Housing Finance Agency, "2010–2011 Enterprise Housing Goals; Enterprise Book-entry Procedures," 75 Federal Register 55892-55939, September 14, 2010; Federal Housing Finance Agency, "2012-2014 Enterprise Housing Goals," 77 Federal Register, , 34263-34281, June 11, 2012.

Note: Alternatively, Fannie Mae and Freddie Mac can meet their housing goals by purchasing mortgages to equal or exceed the market percentage.

Do Fannie Mae and Freddie Mac Have Any Programs to Help Mortgage Borrowers?

Fannie Mae[39] and Freddie Mac[40] each have special programs for mortgage borrowers, but only for borrowers whose loans each holds. These programs include allowing certain borrowers who owe more than their homes are currently worth to refinance their mortgages or enter into repayment plans, forbearance plans, mortgage modifications, and deed-for-lease[41] plans. There are also programs to avoid foreclosure through short sales and deeds-in-lieu of foreclosure.[42]

Fannie Mae and Freddie Mac have programs to allow a homeowner facing foreclosure to surrender the deed in lieu of foreclosure and then to lease the home back.

The Fannie Mae lease is for 12 months and can be renewed, whereas the Freddie Mac lease is month-to-month. Both programs charge a market rate for the lease.

Information on additional government programs is available at http://www.makinghomeaffordable.gov/.

Who Manages the GSEs?

Fannie Mae and Freddie Mac have separate management teams headed by a chief executive officer and overseen by their conservator and regulator, the Federal Housing Finance Agency.

Fannie Mae CEO Daniel H. Mudd and Freddie Mac CEO Richard F. Syron resigned when their companies were placed in conservatorship on September 7, 2008. FHFA appointed Herbert M. Allison Jr. as Fannie Mae's CEO and David Moffett as Freddie Mac's CEO.

Effective March 13, 2009, Moffett resigned from Freddie Mac to return to the private sector. He has since returned as a consultant. On April 20, 2009, Allison resigned from Fannie Mae to accept the nomination to be assistant treasury secretary for financial stability (who oversees Treasury's Troubled Asset Relief Program) and counselor to the Secretary.

On May 10, 2012, Freddie Mac's Board of Directors (with FHFA approval) appointed Donald H. Layton as CEO effective May 21.[43] On June 5, 2012, Fannie Mae's Board of Directors (with FHFA approval) appointed Timothy J. Mayopoulos as CEO effective June 18.[44]

What Is Happening to Executive Compensation?

The Housing and Economic Recovery Act (HERA; P.L. 110-289) strengthened FHFA's regulation over executive compensation and so-called golden parachutes. The senior preferred stock agreement signed by each GSE with FHFA requires the GSEs to get approval for new compensation agreements with executives. The current CEOs each are receiving base salaries of $500,000,[45] but some executives are receiving compensation at higher rates established under previous FHFA-approved agreements.

What is the Difference Between the Housing and Economic Recovery Act of 2008 and the Federal Housing Finance Regulatory Reform Act of 2008?

The Housing and Economic Recovery Act of 2008 is the popular title of the entire law, P.L. 110- 289. The Federal Housing Finance Regulatory Reform Act of 2008 is the popular title for Division A of P.L. 110-289.

FUTURE

Could the GSEs Return to Stockholder Control?

In principle, Congress might decide that the changes that FHFA is making to each of the GSEs reduce the risk of future financial problems to an acceptable level and that the GSEs could return to stockholder control.[46]

The federal government's financial support extended to the GSEs could, however, make a return to the prior status problematic. The elimination of dividends greatly reduced the value of the GSEs' preferred stock. Because the appeal of preferred stock is centered on the security of its dividend payments, the long-run value of the GSEs' preferred stock has been reduced. The value of common stock has been reduced because of the termination of their dividends and increased uncertainty over the future long-run viability of the enterprises. Even if the GSEs were to return to stockholder control, it is not clear how much appeal their common and preferred stock would have for investors. If the GSEs were unable to raise capital, they would be unable to continue.

The treatment of bondholders could make lending to the GSEs more attractive. While common and preferred stockholders suffered during conservatorship (but no more than they would have suffered from dissolution of the GSEs), payments to bond and MBS holders have continued as contracted. The government's actions could convince bondholders that the risk of holding bonds is less than previously thought. This would allow the GSEs to borrow money by selling bonds at rates very close to Treasury rates.

As the housing market fully recovers, the GSEs could be in a very strong position to purchase mortgages and to create MBSs. For stockholders, the economics of the GSEs' mortgage business could be attractive, but the psychology of the decline in stock prices and the federal government's claim on all profits could potentially offset this plus.

One open question in the GSEs' return to stockholder ownership is the government's decision on what to do with the warrants for nearly 80% of the GSEs' ownership. The government could auction the warrants off to the highest bidder, or the government could exercise the warrants to obtain control of the GSEs as each one's majority stockholder.

What Has Conservatorship Done to Stockholders and Other Stakeholders?

The powers of common stockholders, who formerly elected the boards of directors and approved certain enterprise actions, are suspended. FHFA as the conservator has assumed all of their authority. Previously, the common stockholders owned 100% of the GSEs. As a result of the warrants issued to the Treasury, they could own only 20% of the enterprises. In the long run, 20% of a healthy enterprise could be worth more than 100% of GSEs whose liabilities exceed their assets. In the short run, the price of the GSEs' common stock has declined, but if the GSEs recover, stockholders would arguably be better off compared to their situation at the time that conservatorship was undertaken.

To the extent that current and former employees have invested in common stock, in the short run they have seen a decline in the value of their financial assets; the long-run outcome is not clear. Both GSEs had employee stock and option plans. The GSEs' agreements with Treasury prohibit issuing new stock. Consequently, those programs cannot continue until the GSEs emerge from conservatorship.

GSE employees have been urged by FHFA to continue working as before. While the conservator is authorized by federal law to cancel certain contracts, FHFA has said that current contracts continue to be in force.

To keep Fannie Mae and Freddie Mac solvent (assets greater than liabilities), Treasury has purchased special senior preferred stock. The cash paid for the preferred stock is an accounting asset, and the special senior preferred stock increases the Treasury's equity in the GSEs. This senior preferred stock originally paid annual dividends of 10%, which would increase to 12% annually if a GSE fails to pay the dividend; these are the only dividends that the GSEs are allowed to pay.

On August 17, 2012, Treasury signed new agreements with Fannie Mae and Freddie Mac changing the quarterly dividend to be all the profits earned in the quarter. If no profits are earned, no dividend is paid. Treasury said that the purpose of the change was to wind down the GSEs and to benefit taxpayers.[47]

What Are Some of Congress's Options for Restructuring the GSEs?

Going forward, Congress has many options for reorganizing Fannie Mae and Freddie Mac. It could, also, decide to wind down the GSEs and leave the housing market to the private sector. If Congress were to decide to keep and to reorganize Fannie Mae and Freddie Mac, options include (but are not limited to) the following:

- Congress could make Fannie Mae and Freddie Mac part of the government. Both GSEs were originally government corporations, and this would be a return to that environment.
- Fannie Mae and Freddie Mac could become Federal Home Loan Banks. The 12 regional banks are a collective GSE that is owned by their member institutions, and their stock is not publicly traded. Fannie Mae's and Freddie Mac's stock could become an asset of the Federal Home Loan Bank System or of the individual banks.
- Fannie Mae and Freddie Mac could be split up into a large number of GSEs. Instead of two GSEs that are "too big to fail," there would be 10 or some other number of smaller GSEs that would arguably each be small enough to fail. The GSEs could be split in such a way that they would not be clones of each other and one or two could fail without the others going under. Congress might wish to explicitly

state what the risks to stockholders, bondholders, and business partners would be. The competition could mean more benefits from GSE status go to homebuyers instead of the GSEs.

- Fannie Mae and Freddie Mac (and possibly additional new GSEs) could be converted into "utilities." These corporations would not necessarily be GSEs. Each could issue MBSs, possibly guaranteed by the federal government, which would charge a fee for the guarantee. There are a number of options for how the fees could be set. The government could establish a standard fee, or it could auction off the right to issue a specific amount of MBSs. They could sell these MBSs or possibly retain them.
- The government could sell additional new GSE charters to the highest bidders.
- Then-Treasury Secretary Henry M. Paulson Jr. proposed using bonds backed not only by the issuing corporation's legal obligation of repayment, but also by the pledge of specific collateral, as a way to allow banks to supplement or even replace the GSEs' role in mortgage markets.[48]

How Can Fannie Mae and Freddie Mac Leave Conservatorship?

There are two ways that Fannie Mae and Freddie Mac could exit their conservatorships. If they become financially viable, they could return to stockholder control. If they are unable to become financially viable, they could enter receivership. There is no legal reason that one GSE could not go into receivership and the other GSE return to stockholder control, although this might present some policy questions about the desirability of having a monopoly GSE.

There are several obstacles to a return to financial viability. In conservatorship, the GSEs are balancing their goals of support for home mortgage markets and their goal of profitability. At times, these goals may conflict. The concern of the federal government and FHFA for mortgage market stability and liquidity may take precedence over the return to profitability.[49]

Paying the federal government all profits earned in a quarter might prevent the GSEs from accumulating funds to redeem the senior preferred stock. However, if this payment applies only at the *end* of a quarter, it would appear that the GSEs could redeem some senior preferred stock using funds available *before* the end of each quarter. This would be a way for the GSEs could return to stockholder control, although it would likely take many years. FHFA could prevent (or authorize) this redemption of senior preferred stock.

CONTEXT

What Is Conservatorship?

Conservatorship of Fannie Mae and Freddie Mac involves FHFA taking control of the GSEs. As conservator, the powers of the board of directors, officers, and shareholders are transferred to FHFA. A conservator can also cancel certain contracts.

Conservatorship is authorized by the Housing and Economic Recovery Act of 2008 (HERA).[50] The goal of conservatorship is to preserve each of the GSE's assets and to return it to sound financial condition that would allow the conservatorship to be ended.

Who Heads FHFA?

On August 6, 2009, FHFA Director James B. Lockhart announced that he would resign in the near future. President Obama named Senior Deputy Director for Housing Mission and Goals Edward J. DeMarco as acting director.

On November 12, 2010, President Obama nominated Joseph A. Smith, North Carolina commissioner of banks, to be the FHFA director,[51] but the full Senate did not vote on his confirmation. The President has not made another nomination for the position.

Were There Precedents for Placing Fannie Mae and Freddie Mac Under Conservatorship?

This is the first time that a GSE has been placed under conservatorship. It appears to also be the first time that the federal government has made a continuing commitment to a company (other than government corporations). On a more general level, the federal government has intervened in the past to assist many companies.[52] Since placing Fannie Mae and Freddie Mac under conservatorship, the federal government has intervened to support numerous companies, including General Motors, Chrysler, AIG, and various banks.[53]

Why Did FHFA Place Fannie Mae and Freddie Mac Under Conservatorship?

As regulator of Fannie Mae and Freddie Mac, FHFA announced that it had placed Fannie Mae and Freddie Mac under conservatorship because of their deteriorating financial positions and the "critical importance" that each company has to the continued functioning of the residential financial markets.[54]

FHFA has said that continuing audits of the GSEs determined that their financial positions were weaker than previously thought and that the GSEs were unlikely to survive without conservatorship. FHFA cited previous public statements that the GSEs needed to increase their capital and needed to strengthen management controls over operations.

Why Did FHFA Act on September 7, 2008, Instead of Earlier or Later?

FHFA, in general, followed the same approach that the Federal Deposit Insurance Corporation (FDIC) uses when it places a bank in conservatorship: a series of requests for changes to the corporation and to increase capital followed by a sudden takeover. Providing a deadline could provide the regulated entity with an incentive to take risky gambles in a last attempt to avoid being seized by the government. The FDIC usually seizes a bank by suddenly showing up on a Friday afternoon, closing the bank, and locking the doors. This gives the FDIC time to make necessary changes over the weekend and resume business operations on the next business day.

According to media reports at the time, some large foreign investors had been reducing their holdings of GSE debt, MBSs, and stock.[55] This would have made it more difficult for the GSEs to borrow money to finance their portfolios going forward. For example, Bank of China Ltd. is reported to have sold or not replaced $4.6 billion of maturing GSE debt, which reduced its GSE debt holdings to $17.3 billion as of June 30, 2008. These same media reported that Treasury officials contacted foreign central banks and others to reassure them of the creditworthiness of GSE debt.

What Was Fannie Mae's and Freddie Mac's Financial Position?

In placing the GSEs under conservatorship, their new regulator, FHFA, said that they needed assistance to survive. FHFA reported that changes in the economy and the GSEs' slow recovery from their earlier accounting and financial problems reduced their financial strength.[56]

The Office of Federal Housing Enterprise Oversight (OFHEO), which had been Fannie Mae's and Freddie Mac's safety and soundness regulator before July 30, 2008, repeatedly said that the GSEs had adequate capital.[57] In other words, according to OFHEO, the GSEs had sufficient funds to survive their financial difficulties. Because details of the GSEs' portfolios and guarantees include confidential and proprietary information, it is difficult to reconcile the two different assessments of the GSEs' financial position. In broad terms, the GSEs purchased slightly more than $169 billion of private label subprime MBSs in 2006 and 2007; they purchased slightly less than $58 billion of Alt-A MBSs in the same time period, out of combined total mortgage purchases of $1.677 trillion.[58] At the end of 2007, the subprime and Alt-A MBSs represented 13.5% of the GSEs' total assets.

Why Did Fannie Mae's and Freddie Mac's Stock Prices Decline in 2008?

Fannie Mae and Freddie Mac are GSEs whose charters limit them to buying single family and multifamily home mortgages originated by others. This lack of diversification makes them more exposed to housing and mortgage market problems than other financial institutions such as commercial banks, which have other lines of business. The GSEs' charters give them a special relationship with the federal government, sometimes called an implicit guarantee, which has allowed them to borrow at interest rates only slightly above those paid by the federal government. In conservatorship, the GSEs have an even closer connection with the government.

The two GSEs were and are very highly leveraged versions of banks: they borrow money to purchase mortgages, and they maximize profits by keeping their capital reserves close to the minimum required by their regulators. Like banks, the GSEs are required by law and by their regulators to maintain a certain ratio between their loans and reserves to protect against loan losses. A key component of reserves is shareholders' equity or the current value of the shareholders' investments. Using funds for capital provides safety, but it is less profitable in normal times than purchasing additional mortgages.

Changes in the perception of the risks that Fannie Mae and Freddie Mac faced—in terms of future profitability and even continued financial viability—reduced the price that investors were willing to pay for a share of the enterprises. There was also concern that intervention by the federal government would reduce the value of the common stock.

Between the end of 2007 and August 1, 2008, Fannie's stock lost 72% of its value, while Freddie's fell by 77%. Between the end of 2007 and September 30, 2008, Fannie Mae's market capitalization fell from $38.8 billion to $825 million, and Freddie Mac's capitalization declined from $26.8 billion to $473 million.[59] As part of Treasury's financial aid package of September 7, 2008, the GSEs agreed to issue warrants to the Treasury worth 79.9% of their outstanding stock. If Treasury were to exercise the warrants, current stockholders would own 20% of each enterprise instead of 100%. This is one explanation why the GSEs' stock prices declined further since September 7, 2008.

What Had Congress Done Previously to Improve the Financial Condition of the GSEs?

Congress had previously assisted GSEs that were in financial difficulty. When Fannie Mae was losing significant amounts of money in 1982, Congress passed the Miscellaneous Revenue Act of 1982 that provided tax benefits for Fannie Mae.[60] The Farm Credit System, another GSE, was aided by the Agricultural Credit Act of 1987, which authorized the issuance of $4 billion in bonds to support system members.[61]

Section 1117 of HERA authorizes the Treasury to purchase any amount of GSE securities—debt or equity—if necessary to provide stability to financial markets, prevent disruptions in the availability of mortgage credit, or protect the taxpayer.[62] This means that if either of the two GSEs became unable to raise funds in private markets, the federal government could purchase the debt securities that the firms were unable to sell elsewhere, or could recapitalize either firm by purchasing stock, possibly becoming the majority shareholder.

These contracts sent a signal to the markets that the Treasury was prepared to intervene rather than let either GSE fail.

What Other Actions Has the Federal Government Taken to Address the Financial Condition of the GSEs?

On July 15, 2008, the SEC issued an emergency order restricting short selling in the stock of 19 financial institutions, including Fannie and Freddie.[63] The SEC acted to prevent the possibility that false rumors could drive share prices down and cause the market to lose confidence, thereby cutting off the firms' access to credit markets, as happened to Bear Stearns in March 2008. The order restricting short sales of Fannie Mae and Freddie Mac stock was renewed on July 29, 2008, and expired on August 12, 2008.

The government has also taken steps to prepare for possible future support for the GSEs. On July 13, 2008, the Federal Reserve Board of Governors granted the New York Fed the authority to lend directly to the GSEs.[64] Section 1118 of HERA requires the new GSE regulator to consult with the Fed to ensure financial market stability.

In addition to the Fed's existing general authority to be a lender of last resort, the GSEs' charters give the GSEs a special relationship to the nation's central bank.[65] The Fed can use the GSEs' bonds purchased on the secondary market for open market operations.[66] These bond purchases could indirectly help the GSEs by adding to the demand for their debt and increasing their liquidity. The Fed announced that it would conduct a special program to purchase GSE debt and MBSs in calendar 2009 and the first quarter of 2010.[67] Under this program, the Fed purchased more than $1 trillion of GSE debt and GSE-issued MBSs.

In programs that started in September 2008 and ended in March 2010, the Fed and Treasury together purchased $1,135.9 billion in MBSs.[68] On September 21, 2011, the Fed decided to begin reinvesting MBS principal repayments in other MBSs.[69] As of the end of the second quarter of 2012, the Fed held $855.0 billion of Fannie Mae's and Freddie Mac's MBSs.[70]

Who Has Invested in the Fannie Mae and Freddie Mac?

There is little information available about who holds GSE stock, bonds, and MBSs. The Fed reports statistics for combined ownership of government agency and GSE debt and GSE MBSs. At the first quarter of 2012, non-U.S. investors held $999 billion of $7.5 trillion agency and GSE securities.[71] Other large investors were U.S.-chartered depository institutions ($1.7 trillion), life insurance companies ($387 billion), state and local government retirement funds ($290 billion), mutual funds ($1.0 trillion), and the GSEs themselves ($348 billion).

Fannie Mae reports that central bank ownership of certain types of debt declined from 41.1% at the end of 2008 to 15.6% as of May 21, 2012.[72] Freddie Mac showed central bank ownership of its debt declined from slightly less than 40% of the outstanding debt at the end of 2008 to 28% as of May 31, 2012.[73]

What Recent Legislation Has Affected the GSEs?

Since the 110th Congress, five bills and two continuing resolutions have been signed into law that have had significant impacts on Fannie Mae, and Freddie Mac. (See *Table 5.)*

In the 112th Congress, several bills, which have not become law, have been introduced to reform the GSEs. In addition, other legislation, has been introduced to permit the GSEs to purchase larger mortgages.

Table 5. Public Laws Specifically Affecting GSEs (passed in 110th, 111th, and 112th Congresses)

P.L. Number	Date Enacted	Title	Summary
P.L. 110-185	February 13, 2008	Economic Stimulus Act of 2008 (ESA)	Increased conforming loan limits in highcost areas for mortgages originated between July 1, 2007 and December 31, 2008.
P.L. 110-289	July 30, 2008	Housing and Economic Recovery Act of 2008 (HERA)	Created Federal Housing Finance Agency to replace Office of Federal Housing Enterprise Oversight and the Department of Housing and Urban Development as

P.L. Number	Date Enacted	Title	Summary
			combined GSE regulator. Made high-cost area conforming loan limits permanent, but at lower amounts
P.L. 111-5	February 7, 2009	American Recovery and Reinvestment Act of 2009 (ARRA)	Extended 2008 high-cost conforming loan limits to 2009 mortgages.
P.L. 111-88	October 30, 2009	Department of Interior Appropriations Act for FY2010	Extended 2008 high-cost conforming loan limits for FY2010.
P.L. 111-242	September 30, 2010	Continuing Appropriations Act of 2011	Extended 2008 high-cost conforming loan limits for FY2011.
P.L. 112-78	December 23, 2011	Temporary Payroll Tax Cut Continuation Act of 2011	Requires Fannie Mae and Freddie Mac to increase their guarantee fees by 10 basis points. The funds raised are to be deposited in the Treasury.
P.L. 112-105	April 4, 2012	Stop Trading on Congressional Knowledge Act of 2012	Prohibition on bonuses to executives of Fannie Mae and Freddie Mac while they are in conservatorship.

Source: Congressional Research Service.

Glossary

Agency bonds - In this report, agency bonds are those issued by Fannie Mae, Freddie Mac, and Ginnie Mae. Fannie Mae and Freddie Mac are stockholder-owned government-sponsored enterprises. Ginnie Mae is part of the Department of Housing and Urban Development.

Alt-A mortgage - Either a mortgage made to a borrower with a credit history between prime and subprime, or a mortgage made to a prime borrower with less than traditional documentation.

ARRA - American Recovery and Reinvestment Act of 2009, P.L. 111-5, 123 Stat. 115.

ESA - Economic Stimulus Act of 2008, P.L. 110-185, 122 Stat. 613,

FHFA - Federal Housing Finance Agency. Regulator of housing GSEs for mission, safety and soundness. Created by merger of existing government agencies, including OFHEO and HUD staff (who formerly had mission regulatory authority).

GSE - Government-sponsored enterprise.

GSECF - Government-sponsored enterprise credit facility. The Treasury's program to lend money to Fannie Mae, Freddie Mac, and the Federal Home Loan Banks using MBSs as collateral. This program expired December 31, 2009, and had been authorized by HERA.

HERA - Housing and Economic Recovery Act of 2008, P.L. 110-289, 122 Stat. 2654.

MBSs - Mortgage-backed securities. A pool of mortgages sold to institutional investors.

OFHEO - Office of Federal Housing Enterprise. Safety and soundness regulator for Fannie Mae and Freddie Mac. Merged into Federal Housing Finance Agency.

Prime mortgage - A mortgage made to a borrower with excellent credit history.

Private-label MBSs - Mortgage-backed securities underwritten and sold by commercial and investment banks. They are not created by the GSEs or a government agency.

Senior preferred stock This stock is senior to (has priority over) all other common and preferred stock; it is the only GSE stock currently receiving dividends.

Subprime mortgage - A mortgage made to a borrower with a blemished credit history.

End Notes

[1] Michael P. Malloy, The Regulation of Banking: Cases and Materials on Depository Institutions and Their Regulators, (Cincinnati: Anderson Publishing Company, 1992), p. 381.

[2] See Carrie Stradley Lavargna, Government Sponsored Enterprises are "Too Big to Fail:" Balancing Public and Private Interests, 44 Hastings L.J. 991, 998 (1993).

[3] 48 Stat. 1246.

[4] The National Housing Act of 1954, P.L. 83-560, Title II.

[5] The Housing and Urban Development Act of 1968, P.L. 90-448.

[6] The Emergency Home Finance Act, P.L. 91-351.

[7] The Financial Institutions Reform, Recovery, and Enforcement Act of 1989, P.L. 101-73.

[8] CRS Report RS22172, The Conforming Loan Limit, by N. Eric Weiss and Sean M. Hoskins.

[9] Federal Housing Finance Agency, Report to Congress: 2011, pp. 72 and 89, available at http://www.fhfa.gov/ webfiles/24009/FHFA_RepToCongr11_6_14.pdf.

[10] Other major factors associated with high losses to mortgage lenders include loans that do not make any monthly repayment of principal, and mortgages with relatively small downpayments to borrowers with weak credit histories. See, for example, Fannie Mae, "Fannie Mae 2012 Second-Quarter Credit Supplement," August 8, 2012, p. 6, available at http://www.fanniemae.com/resources/file/ir/pdf/quarterly-annual-results/ 2012/ q22012 _credit_summary.pdf.

[11] Although the names prime and subprime suggest that a mortgage should be in one category or the other, the common industry use of prime, Alt-A, and subprime does not have any overlap in the three mortgage categories.

[12] Ibid., p. 78.

[13] Ibid., p. 95.

[14] Fannie Mae, 2012 Second-Quarter Credit Supplement, August 8, 2012, p. 8, available at http://www.fanniemae.com/ resources/file/ir/pdf/quarterly-annual-results/2012/q22012 _credit_summary. pdf, and Freddie Mac, Second Quarter 2012 Financial Results Supplement, August 7, 2012, p. 26, available at http://www.freddiemac. com/investors/ er/pdf/ supplement_2q12.pdf. FICO is a company that provides credit scoring services to lenders.

[15] FHFA, "Data as of August 8, 2012 on Treasury and Federal Reserve Purchase Programs for GSE and Mortgage-Related Securities," available at http://www.fhfa.gov/Default.aspx? Page=70.

[16] Federal Housing Finance Agency, "Data as of August 8, 2012, on Treasury and Federal Reserve Purchase Programs for GSE and Mortgage-Related Securities," available at http: //www.fhfa.gov/Default.aspx?Page=70.

[17] Federal Reserve Bank of New York, "FAQs: Reinvestments of Principal Payments on Agency Securities into Agency MBS," September 26, 2011, available at http://www.newyorkfed. org/markets/ambs/ambs_faq.html.

[18] Federal Reserve Bank of New York, "System Open Market Account Holdings: Securities Holdings as of June 27, 2012," available at http://www.newyorkfed.org/markets/ soma/sysopen_accholdings.html.

[19] Department of Treasury, "Treasury Department Announces Further Steps to Expedite Wind Down of Fannie Mae and Freddie Mac," press release, August 17, 2012, available at http://www.treasury.gov/press-center/press-releases/ Pages/tg1684.aspx. The press release contains links to the amended agreements.

[20] The Economic Stimulus Act of 2008, P.L. 110-185, 122 Stat. 613.

[21] Federal Housing Finance Agency, Report to Congress: 2011, pp. 30-36 and 46-51, available at http://www.fhfa.gov/ webfiles/24009/FHFA_RepToCongr11_6_14.pdf.

[22] A derivative is a financial contract whose value is linked to another financial instrument, price, or variable. For example, two companies could trade a derivative whose value was linked to the difference in the interest rates on 2- year and 10-year Treasury bonds.

[23] Board of Governors of the Federal Reserve System, "Federal Reserve Issues FOMC Statement," press release, September 13, 2012, available at http://www.federalreserve.gov/ newsevents/press/monetary/20120913a.htm.

[24] Board of Governors of the Federal Reserve System, "Current FAQs: What is the Federal Reserve's Maturity Extension Program?" press release, September 21, 2011, available at http://federalreserve.gov/faqs/money_15070.htm.

[25] The Office of Management and Budget (OMB) records only cash transfers between the Treasury and the two GSEs as costs. CBO uses a "fair-value" approach to estimate subsidy costs, which represent "the up-front payment that a private entity in an orderly transaction would require to assume the federal responsibilities for the GSEs' obligations." Another alternative would be to use the cost methods under the Federal Credit Reform Act of 1990, which are used for most federal loan guarantee programs and discounts projected cash flows using interest rates on Treasury obligations. Fair-value estimates use risk-adjusted interest rates.

[26] Federal Housing Finance Agency, "FHFA Updates Projections of Potential Draws for Fannie Mae and Freddie Mac," press release, October 27, 2011, available at http://www.fhfa.gov/webfiles/22737/GSEProjF.pdf.

[27] Congressional Budget Office, The 2012 Long-Term Budget Outlook, June 2012, p. 23, available at http://www.cbo.gov/sites/default/files/cbofiles/attachments/LTBO_One-Col_2.pdf and references therein.

[28] Daniel E. Teclaw and Vandana Sharma, "U.S. Government Cost To Resolve And Relaunch Fannie Mae And Freddie Mac Could Approach $700 Billion," Standard & Poor's, November 4, 2010, p. 1, available at http://www2.standardandpoors.com/spf/pdf/events/FITcon11410Article4.pdf.

[29] Department of Treasury, "Treasury Issues Update on Status of Support for Housing Programs," December 24, 2009, available at http://www.treasury.gov/press-center/press-releases/Pages/200912241534592543.aspx.

[30] More precisely, each the remaining balance of each GSE's $200 billion will be reduced by the positive net worth of the GSE on December 31, 2012.

[31] The American Recovery and Reinvestment Act of 2009, P.L. 111-5, §1117.

[32] Department of Treasury, "Fact Sheet: GSE Mortgage Backed Securities Purchase Program," September 9, 2008, available at http://www.treasury.gov/press-center/press-releases/Documents/mbs_factsheet_090708hp1128.pdf.

[33] Federal Reserve Bank of New York, FAQs: MBS Purchase Program, March 24, 2009, available at http://www.newyorkfed.org/markets/mbs_FAQ.HTML.

[34] Federal Reserve Bank of New York, "Statement Regarding Transactions in Agency Mortgage-Backed Securities and Treasury Securities," September 13, 2012, available at http://www.newyorkfed.org/markets/opolicy/ operating_policy_120913.html.

[35] Department of Treasury, "Fact Sheet: Government Sponsored Enterprise Credit Facility," September 7, 2008, available at http://www.treasury.gov/press-center/press-releases/Documents/gsecf_factsheet_090708.pdf.

[36] CRS Report RL34657, Financial Institution Insolvency: Federal Authority over Fannie Mae, Freddie Mac, and Depository Institutions, by David H. Carpenter and M. Maureen Murphy, contains more information on this subject.

[37] Ben Protess and Azam Ahmed, "Ex-Chief of Freddie May Face Civil Action," The New York Times, March 16, 2011, p. B1.

[38] Of course, Fannie Mae or Freddie Mac's success in meeting or exceeding the mortgage market's percentages in the various goals can only be known after the year is over. This does, however, provide a way to meet the goal requirements if changes in the mortgage market make meeting the goals in Table 3 very difficult or impossible.

[39] Fannie Mae, "Avoiding Foreclosure," available at http://www.fanniemae.com/portal/helping-homeownerscommunities/foreclosure-help.html.

[40] Freddie Mac, "Alternatives to Foreclosure," available at http://www.freddiemac.com/avoidforeclosure/ alternatives_to_foreclosure.html.

[41] In a deed-for-lease plan, the delinquent homeowner surrenders the deed to the lender and leases (rents) the home for an agreed-upon time period.

[42] In a short sale, the lender agrees to cancel a mortgage in return for the proceeds from the sale of a home, even though the proceeds are less than the amount owed. A deed in lieu is when the home owner turns the property over to the lender and is released from the mortgage obligations. In both cases, the lender owns the house, the homeowner moves, and the mortgage is cancelled.

[43] Federal Home Loan Mortgage Corporation, "Form 8-K," May 10, 2012, available at http://www.sec.gov/Archives/ edgar/data/1026214/000102621412000051/f71884e8vk.htm.

[44] Federal National Mortgage Association, "Form 8-K," June 5, 2012, available at http://www.sec.gov/Archives/edgar/ data/310522/000129993312001410/htm_45294.htm.

[45] FHFA, "FHFA Announces New Conservatorship Scorecard for Fannie Mae and Freddie Mac; Reduces Executive Compensation," press release, March 9, 2012, available at http://www.fhfa.gov/webfiles/23438/ExecComp3912F.pdf.

[46] For details on changes at Fannie Mae and Freddie Mac see Federal Housing Finance Agency, Report to Congress: 2011, pp. 21-52, available at http://www.fhfa.gov/webfiles/24009/FHFA_RepToCongr11_6_14.pdf.

[47] Department of Treasury, "Treasury Department Announces Further Steps to Expedite Wind Down of Fannie Mae and Freddie Mac," press release, August 12, 2012, available at http://www.treasury.gov/press-center/press-releases/ Pages/tg1684.aspx.

[48] Henry M. Paulson Jr., Secretary of the Treasury, "Remarks by Secretary Henry M. Paulson Jr. on Recommendations from the President's Working Group on Financial Markets," press release, March 13, 2008, available at http://www.treasury.gov/press-center/press-releases/Pages/hp872.aspx. For more information about covered bonds, see CRS Report R41322, Covered Bonds: Issues in the 112th Congress, by Edward V. Murphy.

[49] Freddie Mac, Form 10-K for the Fiscal Year Ending December 31, p. 19, available at http://www.freddiemac.com/ investors/er/pdf/10k_031109.pdf, and Fannie Mae, Form 10-K for the Fiscal Year Ending December 31, 2008, p. 9, available at http://www.fanniemae.com/ir/pdf/earnings/2008/form10k_022609.pdf.

[50] The Housing and Economic Recovery Act of 2008, P.L. 110-289, 122 Stat. 2654 et seq.

[51] The White House, Office of the Press Secretary, "President Obama Announces More Key Administration Posts," press release, November 12, 2010, available at http://www.whitehouse.gov/the-press-office/2010/11/12/presidentobama-announces-more-key-administration-posts.

[52] CRS Report RL34423, Government Interventions in Financial Markets: Economic and Historic Analysis of Subprime Mortgage Options, by N. Eric Weiss, discusses some of these actions.

[53] CRS Report RS22956, The Cost of Government Financial Interventions, Past and Present, by Baird Webel, Marc Labonte, and N. Eric Weiss; also CRS Report R41427, Troubled Asset Relief Program (TARP): Implementation and Status, by Baird Webel.

[54] FHFA, "Statement of FHFA Director James B. Lockhart," September 7, 2008, available at http://www.fhfa.gov/ webfiles/23/FHFAStatement9708final.pdf. See, also, Henry M. Paulson Jr., On the Brink: Inside the Race to Stop the Collapse of the Global Financial System (New York: Business Plus, 2010).

[55] Deborah Solomon, Michael Corkery, and Liz Rappaport, "Mortgage Bailout Is Greeted With Relief, Fresh Questions," Wall Street Journal, September 9, 2008, p. A1.

[56] Ibid.

[57] OFHEO, "Statement of OFHEO Director James B. Lockhart," July 10, 2008, available at http://www.fhfa.gov/ webfiles/1503/71008Statement.pdf.

[58] OFHEO, Annual Report to Congress: 2008, pp. 113 and 116. Subprime and Alt-A MBS purchases prior to 2006 are not available.

[59] Federal Housing Finance Agency, Report to Congress: 2011, pp. 121 and 138 available at http://www.fhfa.gov/ webfiles/24009/FHFA_RepToCongr11_6_14.pdf.

[60] The Miscellaneous Revenue Act of 1982, P.L. 97-362, 96 Stat. 1726.

[61] The Agricultural Credit Act of 1987, P.L. 100-233, 101 Stat. 1568.

[62] The Housing and Economic Recovery Act of 2008, P.L. 110-289, Sec. 117.

[63] Securities and Exchange Commission, "Emergency Order Pursuant to Section 12(k)(2) of the Securities Exchange Act of 1934 Taking Temporary Action to Respond to Market Developments," available at http://www.sec.gov/rules/ other/2008/34-58166.pdf.

[64] Federal Reserve Board of Governors, "Authority to Lend to Fannie Mae and Freddie Mac," press release, July 13, 2008, available at http://www.federalreserve.gov/newsevents/ press/other/20080713a.htm.

[65] The Fed's lender-of-last-resort authority is delineated at 12 U.S.C. 343. Fannie Mae's charter is at 12 U.S.C. 1716b et seq., and Freddie Mac's charter is at 12 U.S.C. 1401.

[66] 12 U.S.C. 347c.

[67] Federal Reserve Bank of New York, "FAQs: MBS Purchase Program," August 20, 2010, available at http://www.ny.frb.org/markets/mbs_faq.html.

[68] Federal Housing Finance Agency, "Data as of June 10, 2012, on Treasury and Federal Reserve Purchase Programs for GSE and Mortgage-Related Securities," available at http://www.fhfa.gov/webfiles/24022/TSYSupport%202012-06- 20.pdf.

[69] Federal Reserve Bank of New York, "FAQs: Reinvestments of Principal Payments on Agency Securities into Agency MBS," September 26, 2011, available at http://www.newyorkfed. org/markets/ambs/ambs_faq.html.

[70] Federal Reserve Bank of New York, "System Open Market Account Holdings: Securities Holdings as of June 27, 2012," available at http://www.newyorkfed. org/markets /soma/sysopen_accholdings.html.

[71] Federal Reserve, "Agency- and GSE-backed Securities," Flow of Funds Accounts of the United States, June 7, 2012, Table L. 210, available at http://www.federalreserve.gov/ releases/z1/.

[72] Fannie Mae, "Noncallable Benchmark Notes Distribution Reports," Benchmark Securities, YTD 2012, available at http://www.fanniemae.com/resources/file/debt/pdf/benchmark-securities/2012_benchmark_distribution.pdf.

[73] Freddie Mac, Freddie Mac Update, June 2012, available at http://www.freddiemac. com/ investors/pdffiles/investorpresentation.pdf.

INDEX

A

B

C

D

E

F

G

H

I

L

M

N

O

P

Q

R

S

T